Beyond All Reasonable Doubt

At least once in our lifetime
we should all attempt
to evaluate for ourselves
the reality of God.
This is my once.

Dr Michael J Meredith

BOOKS

THE UNIVERSITY OF
WINCHESTER

Copyright © 2002 O Books

Text © 2002 Michael J Meredith

ISBN 0 903816 13 0

Design: Andrew Milne Design

Write to: John Hunt Publishing Ltd,
46A West Street, Alresford,
Hampshire SO24 9AU, UK

A CIP catalogue record for this book is available from the British Library.

Printed in Guernsey, Channel Islands.

Visit us on the Web at: www.o-books.net

Foreword

This book is in every sense the work of a lifetime: it has been long in gestation, certainly, and I have watched with admiration as its argument has been extended and refined over the years. But much more importantly, it is the record of a life seeking understanding. Dr Meredith has a passion for truth, and he movingly tells us of his search for language about God that does justice to both heart and mind.

Like some of the great philosophers of the past, he finds some of his answers by reflecting on the very nature of the mind, leading us to see ourselves afresh. As someone with scientific training, he argues with crispness and vigour. But he always intersperses this with deeply personal testimony. He has a notable feel for words, and readers will treasure some of the phrases he coins ('seeking God is like trying to observe a very shy animal, which only rarely comes to the watering-hole for a drink').

The whole book is really an invitation to the reader to discover for him- or herself how the mind moves us outwards from itself. Because it shows us how to explore our own stories, it has something of the quality not only of an academic argument but of a work of spiritual guidance. Michael Meredith helps us see things through his eyes, with a rare gift of imaginative evocation.

His conclusions are deeply Christian, though none too conventional. His hospitality towards the other great religious traditions of the world is striking; but he works hard to make sense of the belief that in Jesus something of the very heart of the divine mystery is laid bare for all. Like many recent writers, he finds he can best put into words what Jesus makes possible by speaking of our encounter with him as realisation of **being** (some will be reminded of those Eastern icons in which the figure of Jesus is framed with the Greek words meaning 'He who is').

In all, this is a profoundly enriching work, prompting us to discover ourselves and our world in new ways – and to recover the right kind of confidence in our faith: not an arrogant assurance that we have received the key to all knowledge, but the amazed gratitude that a flash of vision has been granted. I hope all his readers will experience something of that vision through this remarkable book.

Rt. Rev. Rowan Williams, Archbishop of Wales

I would like to thank everyone I have ever met
for their contribution to my store of understanding;
in particular I would like to thank Jeanette, my wife.

The most beautiful thing we can experience is the mysterious;
it is the source of all true art and science.
He to whom this emotion is a stranger,
who can no longer pause to wonder and stand rapt in awe,
is as good as dead: his eyes are closed.

Albert Einstein

Preface

I was born into a Christian family. My mother exuded love for me; my father pointed to the majesty of galaxies in the night sky. I first met with God as a three-year-old and with Jesus a few years later. But the light of religious understanding flickered and died in my late teens.

I became a spiritual drifter. At 40, during a period of intense family suffering, I prayed and through my tears I heard God's answer. My spiritual drifting became sincere seeking.

However, as a 'doubting Thomas', I could not convince my restless, turbulent mind to give its full allegiance to God through the love and sacrifice of Jesus Christ. My training as a Professional Chartered Engineer kept calling for objective proof.

I was in my mid-fifties when I finally understood how to express my belief in the universality of God. I knew that God is within, yet beyond, the confines of any particular religious system. At last I had uncovered the *diamond in the mud*.

Over the last decade my need to express my absolute belief in God has intensified. It was early on in this period that a close friend insisted that I write down the thoughts that came to me during my meditations and research. Much later, a group of friendly writers encouragingly pushed me into seeking publication. After much help I was finally led to this publisher.

When our belief in God is challenged we need to know how to respond, with words and actions that resonate with today's technological society. *Beyond All Reasonable Doubt* is the first step in doing just that. It sets out to verify that 'God' is real, countering the claims of those who are deluded into believing that as human beings they are the most advanced knowledge-based processors this universe has to offer. The book reflects my belief that the human condition has meaning far beyond our day-to-day existence.

Contents

Foreword 5

Preface 9

Introduction 13

1. Where Science and Religion Meet 19

    1.1 Science and Faith 19

    1.2 The Experience Spectrum 22

    1.3 Unfolding Truth 28

2. God and the Boundaries of Science 33

    2.1 Science in Practice 33

    2.2 Mathematics and Logic 39

    2.3 The Quantum World 44

    2.4 Cosmology and Creation 48

    2.5 Genetics and the Origin of Life 53

    2.6 Information Technology. 61

    2.7 Seeking the Source 67

3. Approaching God 73

    3.1 Origins 73

    3.2 Evolutionary Limits 79

    3.3 Scriptural Limits 87

    3.4 Looking Inwards 94

    3.5 Seeking Bedrock 100

    3.6 Opening the Door 102

    3.7 Defining an Elementary Experiment 105

3.8 The Apparatus 107

3.9 The Method 110

3.10 Conclusion 115

4. Experiencing God 117

4.1 Introduction 117

4.2 The Subconscious. 121

4.3 Advanced Innovation. 122

4.4 Inspiration. 125

4.5 Simple Visions. 128

4.6 Flowing Empathy. 131

4.7 A Prayer. 135

4.8 Prophesy or Pre-knowledge. 138

4.9 Touching the Infinite. 140

4.10 Assessing Transcendental Experiences 145

5. Aspects of God 149

5.1 Personal - The Gift of Life 149

5.2 Common Pointers to the Existence of God 153

5.3 Possible attributes of God 157

6. Conclusions 161

Further Reading 167

Scriptural 167

General 169

Acknowledgements 173

About the Author 175

Introduction

One of the last things Stella, my mother, asked me was, 'Is there really a God, Mike?' She was 94 years old and a lifelong Christian. My answer, somewhat to my own surprise at the time, was a strong and unequivocal, 'Yes, Mum, there is.'

I believe that there are many today like Stella, who instinctively believe in the reality of God but are lost for words when intellectuals, whether humanists or scientists, argue against the reality of God. There is today a need for bedrock to be established which confirms the existence of God: a verification, independent of any particular religious belief, which does not crumble at the first (or the last) intellectual argument.

That profound, yet simple, question of Stella's is only the beginning, for there are many subsidiary questions concerning the intimacy of God and the underlying purpose of our human condition. Every shade of human belief and religious system will offer us a plethora of solutions to these questions. But before embarking on such 'details', important though they are, it is imperative to *know* that God actually exists.

There are classical theories that claim to verify God's existence in the form of ontological, cosmological, religious or pragmatic arguments and the like. None of these approaches ever fully satisfy me as being an unequivocal truth from which I can *start* my journey of God realisation. I also believe that any understanding of a transcendental existence must consider the complexity of our rapidly changing world brought about by the discoveries of science.

To understand science does not mean that we have to crawl through pages of equations or grasp advanced theories. Much more important is for us to understand the intrinsic limits of science, where it has come from and where it is leading us. We need to extract an understanding of its ultimate boundaries and ascertain if the knowledge of God can be found within these boundaries.

I have found that if we embrace science, instead of shying away from it, we become more focused on its limitations. By exploring the boundaries, or limits, of science we are no longer hoodwinked by arguments which suggest that the ultimate truth of our human existence is to be found in cosmological theories, evolution, genetics, quantum physics, mathematics and the like. We free our minds ready for a fruitful journey into the realms of transcendental truth.

If we wish to analyse anything in conventional science we have to consciously employ the right equipment, the right procedures, and be in the right environment at the right time – so it is when we come to examining the reality of God.

There are many world beliefs that have already provided what they consider to be the right place to experience the transcendental. Some have even placed sumptuous buildings on sacred places (such as great churches, mosques, temples, synagogues, gurdwaras). However, when different groups elaborate on the characteristics of God there is a vast variation of opinion. The history of religion is filled with controversy, perhaps best captured in the *Works of Swami Vivekananda*:

...We find that although there is nothing that has brought to man more blessings than religion, yet at the same time, there is nothing that has brought more horror than religion. Nothing has made more for peace and love than religion; nothing has engendered fiercer hatred than religion. Nothing has made the brotherhood of man more tangible than religion; nothing has bred more bitter enmity between man and man than religion.

Nothing has built more charitable institutions, more hospitals for men and even for animals, than religion; nothing has deluged the world with more blood than religion.

This book is concerned with examining that part of religion which is claimed to be transcendental: in particular the transcendental reality which is often referred to as God.

I can recollect that over 30 years ago when I was in my twenties, I asked a devout member of the Christian church about fundamental aspects of the Jesus story, but he could only say, 'First Mike, you have to believe, then I can explain it all to you.' For me a typical 'chicken and egg' situation. Well I now take it that the chicken is the synonym for God, and God came first. Thus I have spent the intervening years searching for a definitive experiment, which verifies the reality of God. I fully believe that I have found such an experimental procedure, so that now I *know* that God exists. This book sets out to explain how I know.

The first chapter starts our journey by establishing a strong link between science and transcendental experiences. Next we travel to the limits of many scientific theories seeking God. By examining the concepts behind our technological revolution, pointers to the meaning of each of our lives begin to emerge.

Definite support for the hypothesis that God exists can be found through the accumulated knowledge of history and the wisdom of world scriptures, but it is not conclusive. It is only when we embark on a journey, which leads to an understanding of our own personal existence, that the threads begin to converge. I believe that when an individual actively seeks to know that the transcendental truly exists an experiment is possible. The experiment described must be carried out consciously and humbly to expose an inner understanding, a bedrock of truth; a truth that unequivocally points to the existence of a transcendental reality.

This bedrock is in the form of a natural experiment, which enables the experimenter to know that a transcendental dimension exists. It is from this knowledge that God can be realised.

In today's idiom you could say that my mission statement is to firmly establish *Beyond All Reasonable Doubt*, that God actually exists, and begin to answer Bertrand Russell's, 'If he [God] is as real to Christians as he would seem to be, why doesn't he make himself known to the rest of us?'

But, a word of warning from the Gospel of St Matthew, 'Truly I tell you: unless you turn around and become like children, you will never enter the kingdom [of God].'

With love, prayers and peace

Michael

Chapter 1

Where Science and Religion Meet

This chapter sets out to establish a common truth
between worldly and transcendental knowledge.

1.1 Science and Faith

Once I would have taken for granted that the religious system of my birth would ultimately explain everything of importance in my life. Today it often appears that science has replaced those traditional beliefs. Science has broadened and deepened our understanding of the physical envelope in which we live, and has substantially increased our life expectancy. Is it possible for science to ultimately tell me all there is to know? Or is science intrinsically limited?

Science, by definition, is all about what is verifiable and reproducible. It is about proving answers to logical questions, it is about discovering results, which can be analysed by logic, and it is about understanding how the world around us fits together.

Will, then, this 'science stuff' eventually show me the ultimate reason for my existence? Am I simply the result of physical laws and chance? Or am I part of a deeper meaning that is beyond conventional measurement? These are the fundamental questions to which I am seeking the answers. By 'beyond conventional measurement' I mean that which is not recorded by our sense experiences of touch, smell, sight, hearing or taste, and beyond descriptors such as beauty. I want to know if there is a *transcendental reality*, because the transcendental is the core of all religions and is where humankind's knowledge of God is born.

The *transcendental* is a phenomenon, which by its very definition exceeds all conventional understanding. So it should come as no surprise that it is almost impossible to pin down such a concept. A transcendental reality is claimed to be part of all religious belief systems, from Buddhism, Mother Earth and Spirituality to Hinduism and the Creator God popularised in Western culture. It seems to defy all definition and be beyond all names and forms; nevertheless, for me to begin to explore it I must give it a handle, a name. This problem of naming is not new. I recollect reading a second-century writing of the Acts of Thomas in a non-biblical account of the early Christian Church where Thomas (Judas) is grappling with naming this transcendental, this 'beyond' phenomena. He suggested: 'Thou canst not hear his name at this time, but the name which was bestowed upon him for a season is Jesus, the Christ.'

Many have claimed to know the name of the 'beyond' and use words such as - 'Lord God', 'Ultimate Reality', 'Greater Consciousness', 'Great Light', 'Benevolent Altruistic Force', 'Creator God', 'Holy Spirit', 'Allah' and so on. But, 'for a season', to set the ball rolling, I will use the term 'God' for that which may be partly accessible, but in totality will always be beyond human knowledge and understanding. God could, in one sense, be thought to be the 'transcendental motivation' behind all that exists.

On the other hand, is science proving that all our 'of God' experiences are nothing more than brain activity?

Recent studies of the brain suggest that some qualities of the mind now seem to be surprisingly mechanistic. Neurologists at the University of California in San Diego have located an area in the brain, a 'God-Spot', that appears to produce intense feelings of mysticism, transcendence and even a sense of a 'presence'.

The Canadian neuroscientist Michael Persinger, of Laurentian University, has stimulated the 'God-Spot' in non-believers, and reported, 'Typically people report a presence. One time we had a strobe light going and this individual actually saw Christ in the strobe.'

I am interested in relating such exciting discoveries as these to my understanding of the reality of God, for, as we shall discover, these things are far from incompatible.

It is still widely believed today that, whereas science is logical and rational, mankind's understanding of God is founded on unsubstantiated emotion. This separation of science from spiritual beliefs is firmly rooted in medieval philosophers such as Thomas Aquinas who suggested that, 'Science and faith cannot co-exist in the one person...' But are the scientific and the transcendental so completely different?

Before making further progress, there is a need to know if science and any possible transcendental phenomena are, in fact, mutually exclusive. Do they have a hard, unyielding, non-interactive edge between them? Or is there a seamless continuum between science and the transcendental? To answer such questions it is important to carefully examine both, to see if there are any detectable underlying patterns. In the next section we will investigate how scientific facts emerge from experience, and then suggest how our everyday experiences could, in fact, be pointers to a reality that is of a transcendental nature.

1.2 The Experience Spectrum

A scientific 'fact' relies upon accurately predicting some future event by using related previous experience. It is by following the correct procedure that science allows a predictable 'future event' to recur time and time again. The result of any experimental procedure allows us to have practical acquaintance with a series of 'identical' *repeated experiences*.

For example, I could perform a simple 'scientific' experiment such as dropping a crystal wine glass, from a height of three metres onto a solid, inelastic concrete floor. This would result in the crystal glass shattering into a myriad fragments, and this will occur every time I carry out the same procedure. The more times I carry out the 'experiment' the more convinced I become that the crystal glass will always shatter into fragments. And as my experience grows so does my confidence that I can always correctly predict the outcome of this experiment. My confidence is further boosted if I hear of other world famous scientists dropping crystal glasses with the same catastrophic result that I experienced, thus reinforcing my own observations.

In time I become convinced that a glass container subject to my experimental procedure will always break. And I become more and more convinced that what I have observed is a true reflection of a real world event.

At this point, like all good scientists, I will seek to draw as wide a conclusion as possible from my experimental results. I may decide to publish my 'law of bounce-less glass', which I state as, 'any glass container moving beyond a velocity equivalent to that of gravity acting on it over a distance of three metres, which comes into contact with an unyielding body, will always shatter.' And all seems well. But is it? Unbeknown to me there could have been a parallel development of crystal glass which, instead of shattering on impact with any solid body, assumed the properties of a bouncy rubber ball, later to fully regain its original shape and rigidity.

My world renowned 'law of bounce-less glass' would be just another piece of obsolete information scattered along the time-avenue of scientific progress.s

This simplified example is typical of all scientific information and progress, where one 'cast iron' theory is overturned by another. And this will become more apparent when the boundaries of science are discussed in more detail in Chapter 2. The problem lies at the very heart of scientific endeavour with its three distinct paradigms. First there are the initial assumptions (the conditions and environment before, during and after any experiment, along with the properties of the materials used). The second concerns the way in which the experiment is performed and the observations during and after the experiment. While the third is the theories, propositions, hypothesis and projections that result. It is these latter speculations that are all too often taken as being proven. (You may have noticed in the above example that my specific 'crystal glass' experimental results were interpreted in the above 'law' as 'any glass container'. This tendency to turn the specific into the universal is often found in scientific endeavour.) In the great majority of cases 'proven' laws are, in fact, not fundamental truths, but more a case of pointers on the long, long road to uncovering the realities of our physical environment.

It is through one or more of our five sense experiences that all external things, whether scientific or naturally occurring events, are verified. For all realities that occur in or about the universe in which we live are external to our mind. It is when one of our five senses reports to our brain that we become aware of some 'fact' or other. Like seeing or feeling the sunset, hearing thunder, smelling honeysuckle or tasting English mustard. For facts to be scientifically 'proven' they have to be repeatable by anyone who carefully follows a given procedure, so that they too can experience the same result.

What then of other *experiences?* Are they so different from those of scientists in laboratories? Does, for example, an experience of art or music show consistency? Judges in a beauty contest are seldom in full agreement, for everyone knows that 'beauty is in the eye of the beholder'. What then is truth in art or music? Do socially acceptable truths only occur when the majority agree with each other? Much of science, like all human knowledge, is in a continuous state of change because, in any society, truth is in general based upon human agreement rather than absolute truth. When others share in the same opinions as we ourselves do, it causes our *confidence* to increase, not necessarily the ultimate *reality* of our perceived truth. Politicians are very aware of this as was so clearly demonstrated when a certain minister tried to show his child eating a beefburger to convince us all that BSE was under control. He was simply ignoring his lack of knowledge and attempting to increase our confidence in what he wanted us to believe as truthful.

What then of the individual experience? Are all our 'one-off' experiences automatically to be assigned as being false – rubbish to be thrown into the 'dustbin'? Surely I cannot simply call something false because no one else was aware of my experience, or because I am unable to reproduce the experience?

I recollect such a 'one-off' experience that was far from being transcendental or 'of the other world'. It occurred when I was at home in the spring of 1991. At the time I was living in *The Boathouse*, where bedrooms snuggled into the leafy banks of the river Taff, while lounge and dining areas projected into space, held high above the river on sturdy wooden stilts. In the distance were the hilly slopes of Graig Llanishen and the woods of Coed Coesau - gentle hills that hide Caerphilly from the city. From the veranda we had a superb view of such colourful events as the Llandaff Regatta in the summer and the piercing blackness of cormorants as they fished for eels in the quieter moments.

One particular spring morning I was up just before the warm blanketing sun cradled the city in its reassuring orange glow, feeling so very fortunate to live by a river in the beautiful capital city of Wales.

While looking through the window I saw a flash of brilliant blue, which paused briefly on a branch protruding from the water; a kingfisher. A kingfisher that could have hatched near the pure springs of Pen-y-fan, the highest peak in the Brecon Beacons National Park, and then travelled through the heartland of the old industrial South Wales, to stop here, just for me.

The luminous turquoise feathers gave the kingfisher a surreal glow as its keen eyes stared in bewilderment at the murky water. It represented a tangible proof to me that things were changing; the river was slowly clearing its saturated years of grimy industrial pollution to run, once again, free and full of life.

A few months later my sister Joan, and her husband Richard, came over from Bristol for a meal. While talking, the subject of our house nameplate came up and Richard asked why we had chosen a kingfisher as our motif, adding, 'Kingfishers are still quite a rarity, even in the countryside.'

I told him, with somewhat childish pleasure about the kingfisher that I had seen.

'Yes,' he said, 'I've made that kind of mistake myself, seeing a common house sparrow out of the corner of my eye and thinking that it was something quite exotic'.

To my surprise, I could not convince him that a kingfisher had visited our city that spring morning, for I had no proof, no photograph, no carcass.

It seems to me that many one-off experiences can be like my kingfisher, unrepeatable and therefore deemed to be unprovable, and it is very understandable that others who have not experienced them have difficulties in believing in them.

The first swallow swoops from above, diving and shooting past. Was it real, was it a blown leaf, a sparrow, or just a longing thought that flashed through my mind?

'There was no swallow; won't be here for ages; they're still in the mud!' I hear an ancient belief muttered by an old sceptic whose tired eyes missed the dart of beauty, which I knew, was the first swallow. We who perceived, whose experience was so immediately vivid for just one moment, droop, begin to doubt, to lose our confidence and be unsure even when, later on, others say, 'Yes, I saw it too.'

If one-off events are sometimes difficult to believe, then it is understandable that it should be difficult to communicate that one-off experience which could be of a transcendental nature. This is succinctly stated in the Gospel of Saint John where it suggests, 'If you disbelieve me when I talk to you about things on earth, how are you to believe if I should talk about the things of Heaven?'

All experiences, whether of a scientific nature or appreciation of beauty or those which may well turn out to be of the transcendental, are part of the same 'experience spectrum', even if they are at different points on that spectrum.

To sum up: *all* human understanding and acquired facts are through experiences. At one extreme there are the *repeatable* worldly and scientific experiences in which we have great confidence in their absolute reality. Next come a whole gambit of worldly and scientific experiences whose cause and reality is a constant arena for debate. Finally, at the other extreme are the unique 'one-off' experiences which are difficult, or sometimes impossible, to substantiate. It is within these unique, one-off, experiences that leading-edge scientists and all great innovators first realise their inspirations. I myself have been in the position of obtaining perfect results and then spending many frustrating weeks trying to reproduce them. It is also within the individual event that the vast majority of spiritual and transcendental experiences occur. This band of decreasing confidence from the predictable-repeatable to the unique could be thought of as the 'experience spectrum' in which our minds operate.

We are bombarded with countless experiences every day, from the mundane 'washing-up' tasks, to mental insights, which at times can be quite profound. Surrounded with so much information clutter, where do we stand as we search for an ultimate reality?

1.3 Unfolding Truth

Truth could be thought of as being like a huge dark field, stretching further than the mind can perceive. Above the field shine down little cones of light, one cone for each of us. And if we are not careful, we start considering that our understanding, within the confines of our own 'truth cone', is all that exists and we become isolated – not understanding the perspective of our neighbour.

The cone of light that illuminates one person's understanding only allows them to have partial knowledge of the absolute truth plane. For each 'personal truth' is but one little pool of light shining on that infinite, dark plane.

We all live in our little pools of light, sometimes in groups, sometimes alone. From within our 'light pool' it is often very difficult to begin to recognise that others perceive a different world to our own. A different faith or social group appears to see a different truth, even if there is some overlap with our own little pool of knowledge.

Are the options other people give us our complete choice or have these people been simply channelling our minds in a specific way? Take for example that well-known and respected Christian writer C S Lewis. He suggests that Jesus was either 'mad' or 'bad' or 'he was what he said he was'. But are these our only options? What about, for example, verifying the authenticity of the biblical writing itself? *The Jerusalem Bible*, in its introduction to the Synoptic Gospels, suggests,

Neither the apostles themselves, however, nor any of the other preachers of the gospel message and tellers of the gospel story ever aimed at writing or teaching history in the modern technical sense of that word; their concern was missionary and theological: they preached to convert and

edify, to infuse faith, to enlighten it and defend it against its opponents…

This same highly acclaimed and well researched translation of the Bible gives the following footnote when referring to the Gospel of Saint Luke's account of the *Magnificat,*

> *…Mary's canticle [the Magnificat] is reminiscent of Hannah's…and many other biblical 'Old Testament' passages…Luke must have found this canticle in the circles of the 'Poor', where it was perhaps attributed to the Daughter of Zion…*

Where then is truth? Did Mary actually say the *Magnificat* or is it simply the 'poetic licence' of the writer struggling to convey the wonder that she must have felt? I have heard it said by very talented authors, 'at times facts can get in the way of truth.' A sober thought when we take on board that by definition all world scriptures have been written by human hand, no matter how inspired or filled with God the writer might have been. To find out the truth concerning the existence of God, we will have to proceed with extreme caution even when we use our most cherished source of information.

What we believe to be true is greatly influenced by our faith in the integrity of the source of the information. A person's statement about something we cannot see, touch, smell, taste or hear will be viewed according to our knowledge of the person, our rating of his integrity, our knowledge of his personal (and hidden) agenda, as well as our own belief at the time. A literalist who cannot move from established doctrine, will, I believe, soon stray from truth, struggling to justify an exact and unimaginative rendering of a 'fact'. A 'fact', which may have originally been intended to be taken figuratively or metaphorically. Closed minds can be found in all human enterprises from religious fundamentalists to the rigid intellects of some eminent scientists.

The basis of all our judgement is internal; we perceive through our senses; new information is compared with what we already 'know' or believe to be true, and spiced with our own prejudices and gullibility. New knowledge can bring change so that we shift the bases from which we judge in future. As we develop in childhood we learn that certain actions result in consistent rewards or pain. Also we realise that we have often been deceived for many years; *truth* is always to be questioned. The fact that I had to ask my mother, 'Is there really a Father Christmas?' shows me that eventually we even have to doubt a most trusted parent – let alone believing an 'unknown' scientist who insists that GM crops are 'perfectly safe'. A very healthy scepticism evolves within us, which helps us to cope with a deceptive world. Keeping this childish ability to question what appears to be an absolute certainty is the essential ingredient for finding an ultimate reality.

To find truth we must always be open to fresh evidence and willing to change our views under the weight of substantial new information. How are we to react to those recent brain studies that point to us all having a 'God-Spot'? Do we try and ignore them or should we, in faith, consider their implications in our search for the transcendental? I have found the latter to be most profitable and I find that I am in agreement with people such as the medical writer Rita Carter who suggests that, 'After all, if God exists, it figures He must have created us with some biological mechanism with which to apprehend Him.' In other words, finding parts of the body that can be artificially stimulated like a knee-jerk does not imply that the knee does not have a more important function. Try walking!

Perhaps the greatest obstacles to uncovering truth are self-esteem and 'greed'. Loss of self-esteem is mostly feared by those members of society who have much to lose. There are many scriptural references to human ego preventing us seeing God, one of the best summaries I like is from the *Gospel of Ramakrishna*:

A man is able to see God as soon as he gets rid of ego and other limitations. He sees God as soon as he is free from such feelings as 'I am a scholar', 'I am the son of such and such a person', 'I am wealthy', 'I am honourable', and so forth...

We can all so easily become over-concerned about our position in society. Then again, I have met many who are only willing to discuss their initial premise or 'belief' in a superficial way. They seem to be unable to cope with a wider truth and refuse to engage in all concepts that suggest they could be misguided. On the other hand it could be a dullness of mind, apathy or the conflicting cares and needs of daily life that prevents them from examining fresh evidence.

This chapter has been concerned with examining where science and religion meet. Now although it could be said that in essence religious experience, like consciousness, is a first-person phenomenon and science is a third-person phenomenon, nevertheless they are both verified by experience. That is to say, if the transcendental exists, it meets science under the umbrella of human experience, particularly the unique one-off experience. It is one-off experiences that characterise the first blossom of any new discovery in science and, I believe, we will find that it is the one-off experience that will give the greatest possibility of encountering the transcendental, and therefore God. It is in the area of unique experience that we must define and conduct an experiment that aims at verifying, or disproving, the reality of God.
The transcendental and the scientific meet in the confines of unique events. The transcendental can, in some ways, be com-

pared with the innovations that occur at the limits or the frontiers of science.

In the next chapter we will explore the frontiers, or boundaries, of conventional science to see if there is any way we can prove or disprove the reality of God. This will be no easy task, but then, who would consider unravelling anything as complex as verifying the existence of God to be simple? By realising the boundaries of science we will begin to separate out the truths of science, which point to a deeper reality behind our own existence. It is from this latter reality that we can ultimately, with confidence, evaluate the reality of God. In some respects we are seeking 'the back door' into traditional religion by using the key of personal experience.

As we progress it will become more and more apparent that both conventional science and the transcendental have within them areas that can be perceived and experienced. Both also point to that which is immeasurable and incomprehensible.

Chapter 2

God and the Boundaries of Science

This chapter sets out to show the limits of science and to establish useful pointers to that which may be beyond.

2.1 Science in Practice

If you believe that the existence of God is uncertain, it is worth remembering that there is uncertainty in the outcome of even the most trusted scientific achievements. This is even true in technological equipment that has been proven to be reliable for many decades. My first glimpse of the uncertainty inherent in science was back in the 1950s. At the time I was a young professional engineer in the design team for an airborne computer system. Here, to my astonishment and concern, I learned that *failure is built into all design*, and an aeroplane is no exception. For the fact is that to have no risk at all would simply mean no aeroplane.

By today's standards the 1950s technology was quite cumbersome. However, many of the fundamental concepts have remained. When I first came into contact with the flight control computers, or autopilot technology, the discussion went something like this:

Q What will happen if the main computer in the flight control system fails?

A No problem. A second computer would automatically take over.

Q Hang on a minute. How do you know which one is right?

A Easy. In practice the two computers are monitoring the situation and if one deviates in its results compared with the other then one of them must be wrong.

Q Great. But which one?

And so we arrived at the logic of a computer trinity! With three computers it was assumed that if two were predicting the same outcome, and the third was predicting something else then the two, being the majority, were right – a computer democracy.

In practice, wherever possible the aircraft bristled with all forms of triplicate control systems.

By a process of rapid evolution the third computer soon became smaller, lighter and a less expensive device that only needed to monitor critical decisions. All malfunctions were made to be 'fail-soft'; i.e. an equipment failure was designed so that if something did stop functioning properly it would allow the pilots to react before any disaster occurred.

A good example of an early 'fail-soft' system was employed in the British Trident aircraft of the 1960s. In those days high-flying jet aeroplanes had suffered several accidents caused by 'super-stall'. The 'superstall' happens when the plane is flying along with its angle of attack too high for its forward velocity or air speed. This is the situation when the aeroplane is trying to climb faster than its speed will allow – the nose of the aeroplane is pointing up too much. This results in insufficient air being taken in by the jets. The engines experience a flameout and literally stop dead. Consequently the aeroplane, in a 'superstall', falls out of the sky tail first – without power!

To get around this usually fatal problem the ingenious and somewhat simple idea of the stick-shaker was employed. This was a system whereby the pilot's attention was ensured, over and above the instrumentation warnings, by a violent shaking of the control column to indicate that the onboard computers were predicting imminent disaster if the nose of the aircraft was not rapidly pointed downwards.

Ingenuity knew no bounds and it was decided that if the pilot and co-pilot both ignored these warnings a second system would operate which automatically forced the control column forward. This put the plane into a dive and prevented a jet flameout and the resulting 'superstall' conditions from arising. I had the unfortunate experience of being one of the first people to experience the test runs of this device over East Anglia and the North Sea. What started as a super day with a marvellous lunch turned out to be one of the physically sickest of my life as the chief test pilot repeatedly tested and re-tested the device.

All aircraft today have many alternatives designed into their construction, which minimise the possibility of critical accidents occurring. In the real world of science and technology I discovered that there are no absolutes, only probabilities of something being true. Probability also forms part of all production work. Take the manufacture of computer integrated circuits. Although it can be predicted that in any one batch of say 100 sophisticated computer microchips, 95 will be made satisfactory, we cannot know in advance just which five are going to fail. For if it were known the errors could well be avoided.

And now we come to the crux of the matter, that is, that science has great difficulties predicting the outcome of any individual event, be it associated with a microchip or a person.

For example, the medical world is always striving to improve its knowledge. It is well known that individuals react differently when presented with identical drugs or body transplants. Absolute effects are unknown. Traditional medicine is full of best guesses, or calculated risk factors – there are no perfect answers. Early heart transplants resulted in no long-term survivors, whereas by the mid-1990s the chances of survival were around 85 per cent. However, that meant a failure rate of 15 per cent, or about one in seven operations, which depended upon circumstances beyond the existing knowledge of medical staff at the time. At the present time no one can tell you, as an *individual*, exactly what your chances of surviving a heart transplant are. For if it were known that you would not survive the operation there would be no point in giving you a new heart. Consequently the chances of successful operations would increase, although, all other things being equal, the number of deaths would remain unaltered.

Another example is to be found in noise measurement. Is the scientific work in this area factual? Or do feelings and emotions affect the measured results?

In practice the effect of sound varies from being very enjoyable music to causing extreme pain depending upon our expectation, temperament, time of day, sensitivity, and so on. If your neighbours are having a noisy party, you can lodge a legitimate complaint based upon a simple noise measurement. On the other hand, if they had invited you around you could well have enjoyed the excessive volume.

The dysfunction of the human hearing system, tinnitus, results in noises being 'heard' in the brain when there are no external stimuli. In this case the 'pain' experienced by the sufferer is beyond scientific measurement. Although measurement of noises generated within the ear and the auditory nerves may be possible, the pain experienced by the sufferer's mind is impossible to measure in any meaningful way. It may always prove to be unmeasurable, except by resorting to the most fundamental method, that of simply asking the sufferer how loud the noise appears. This is the method employed at present. It allows results to be recorded based upon opinions and personal guesses. Results are recorded on a ten-point scale, using descriptors such as loud, very loud, painful, and so on.

In pain measurements, truth is not absolute; it is relative, and then only relative to the sufferer. Thus it could be that in suffering, one person will decide that, on a scale of 0-10, their discomfort or pain level is ten, and they are becoming suicidal. Whereas another person, with a similar stimulus causing their pain, may say that their discomfort level was at an acceptable four or five. Who is right? Is there a right or a wrong?

There is still another conundrum, for in reality everything that involves science already exists in one form or another. Not even the best scientist can produce anything from nothing at all; therefore it must already exist.

Still, we have come a long way since primitive man first threw a stone or used a stick, so something is going on – something, which affects us every day of our lives. But can we expect scientists who limit themselves to the phenomenal, or worldly, to find out if a non-physical, or transcendental, reality actually exists?

Now is the time to investigate the limits of science and technology, to find boundaries, and so establish whether or not science has the inherent ability to prove or disprove the existence of God. I will have to move with extreme caution when looking for the boundaries of science. I will have to try and sort out 'facts' from the more numerous assertions encountered when scientists start to explain what they have seen and why it occurred. It is not uncommon for scientists to interpret the results of their often well-researched investigations, by using hypotheses, myth, assumption and even a form of what could best be described as 'religious fever', rather than informing us when they leap into their own unfounded 'awesome' prophecies. I prefer the approach of those nineteenth-century discoverers like Newton and Faraday who, despite seeking to discover God's action in the world, uncovered much that underpins the truths of our present day technology.

Many scientists today are blown along on the streams of function, interest, excitement and pride and have, unlike Newton or Faraday, often 'thrown out the baby with the bath water'. One problem with our modern worldview is that many theologians and scientists are unable to cross converse. For it is comparatively easy to become bogged down in theological arguments based upon fossilised premises. For example, is the Bible factual or is it human hopes and desires? Is it God telling humankind something appropriate to their understanding at the time – humanity developing over millennia as children develop over their lifetimes? Both the scientist and the theologian, it seems, can so easily insist on breaking up the spectrum of the understanding and knowledge gained through experience. There should be no insurmountable fence put up between science and religion.

To enter into any possible transcendental reality we may well have to go beyond the boundaries of conventional science. To go beyond the boundaries of conventional science we will have to know just what those boundaries are. To do this I will consider several representative areas of modern science, seeking an overall pattern. These representative areas will cover mathematics, the quanta, the cosmological, genetic life, and information technology. Thus we travel from the evaluation tools of mathematics, through the little and the large elements of our physical environment and our own biological manifestation, to finally address that which underpins our understanding of reality – information itself.

First then, to investigate some ideas found within mathematics and logic.

2.2 Mathematics and Logic

Can we mathematically show that God is unnecessary for the universe to exist? For that matter can anyone even mathematically prove that one plus one equals two? Not demonstrate or illustrate it, but actually prove the truth of it. To date there has never been a watertight theoretical basis or absolute proof of even this most elementary premise of arithmetic. Concepts such as 1+1=2 can only be confirmed through experience, for it is one of the many unprovable starting points, or axioms, required for mathematics to operate at all.

Mathematics is to me a sort of enjoyable miracle. It is a brilliant tool for predicting aspects of the real world. It often seems to be full of mystical power that denies all freedom of choice.

Could an absolute reality be uncovered which points to the truth or otherwise of a transcendental event using a mathematical formula or concept? I fail to see how it could, for mathematics by its very nature is bounded. It ultimately aims at a practical target, such as achieving the theoretical, mathematically derived temperature of absolute zero, a point where all known motion is predicted to cease – a temperature of around –273°C. However, in practice, this could be a temperature that is never quite realised. It reminds me more of a man walking home. On the first day he walks half way. On the second day he is tiring so he only walks half the distance of the first day. He continues to walk half the distance of his previous day forever more, for there is always something left, ensuring that he never actually crosses the threshold. He never actually arrives home. Although absolute zero may be achieved, it seems to me that the predicting power of mathematics is limited, and is more akin to that tired man trying to walk to a place he already knows, rather than absolute reality.

Modern mathematics may have evolved far beyond the orderly world where simple counting, geometry and algebra ruled; even so it cannot get to grips with the complexity of individuality, such as a specific outcome within a group event. It is, for example, unlikely that a computer program will ever be available which unequivocally predicts the winner of the Grand National horse race. This was reinforced for me in the late summer of 1987, when my wife, Jeanette, and I stayed for a week overlooking an island-rich lake just outside Angers in the Loire Valley of France.

In the evening sky, above the lake islands, a cloud composed of thousands of starlings moved in the unison of one flock. The cloud twisted and turned, dived and soared, one homogeneous life form. I picked out the lead bird but within a minute or less a second bird, a 'nobody', from nowhere in particular, led the dance.

Perhaps the leaders rested a while and retook the lead? But not so; over several nights I focused on the leader, after a short span as guide it simply became once more just a common member of the flock. On those clear nights with all my concentration on the temporary leader, I never saw one regain the leadership. It was as if the 'life' of the flock surpassed the individuals within it. The mathematics of the whole is quite different from that of the individual, although the flock is composed of individuals.

I have watched shoals of sardines under the great bridge of Portimao in Portugal, a silver cascading oneness, united yet individual – behaving in the same way as the starlings.

Patterns are everywhere. Patterns that allow us to mathematically model the real world and predict future outcomes. However, the predictions are *possible* outcomes of the general case, not the *actual* outcome itself. Due to the minute randomness that affects the starling flock, mathematics could never predict the exact position of the flock ten seconds into the future. It could, however, with modern mathematics (such as fractals) quite easily reproduce the general movement of the flock by using a computer. General computer simulations of real events may make us feel that we know, we control, simply because we have observed and named the phenomenon – in reality they only highlight our ignorance of *individuality*. Or as Stuart Kauffman, that well-known stalwart of 'artificial life', understandably suggested, 'Individual systems in the ensemble might be very different.'

Mathematics is a specialised and powerful international language that tells much about the universe in which we find ourselves. It is a particular, and therefore limited, way of describing the observed universe. Mathematics is an extension of language itself. It could be thought of as a tool that brings much of our universe into focus, but mathematics is not the universe.

I have witnessed many who successfully invoke infinity, myself included, as a tool to increase scientific knowledge and understanding, but we must remember that infinity *does not exist* in any practical form. Our universe does not, as far as we are able to assess, contain anything that is infinite – all is in fact finite. Invoking mathematical descriptors like 'infinite' may seem to be an excellent way for theologians to describe God, but such an assumption is treading on a very shaky premise indeed. Infinity only exists as a concept, a form of advanced language (mathematics), in the mind of humanity. Once infinity is invoked anything is possible. Even the most well-established scientists make the mistake of extending the theoretical concept of infinity to the real world.

For example, Friedrich Nietzsche suggested, in the nineteenth century, that time is infinite. He went on to assert, from this unverifiable assumption, that all combinations of atoms that could possibly occur, will occur, and what is more they will occur many (an infinite number of) times. Hence, he suggested, we will all occur in our present form again and again and again - an infinite number of lives each, so to speak.

Contemporary cosmologists have explained many ways in which there could be infinite matter. For example, Andrei Linde, who became a professor of physics at Stanford University in 1990, has produced a well-argued case within the 'Inflationary Theory of the Universe' that suggests an infinite number of universes are forever forming by bubbling out of each other. Therefore we exist because, by definition, our universe is that universe that happens to have exactly the right conditions for our evolution - without the need for any intelligence.

Thus, assigning infinity to any variable in any system ensures that everything we humans can ever imagine can be deemed to happen. It is the descriptor, or logic, of infinity that creates such a god, not the system itself.

It becomes obvious that to simply suggest that God has some infinite characteristic or perfection, although the infinite characteristic could be true, in no way aids our case for verifying the existence of God.

Although the concept of infinity exists in the virtual world of mathematics, it does not form part of the real tangible universe in which we find ourselves. Blaise Pascal, the seventeenth-century French mathematician, gave what I consider to be an elegant analogy, when he likened infinity to God,

We know that there is an infinite, and do not know its nature. As we know it to be untrue that numbers are finite, it is therefore true that there is a numerical infinity. But we do not know its nature; it cannot be even and it cannot be odd, for the addition of a unit cannot change it. Nevertheless it is a number, and all numbers are either even or odd. So, we may know that there is a God without knowing what He is.

In the end using mathematics is something like using a convex lens to observe a garden ant and then confusing the image of the ant with the ant itself. Mathematics by its very descriptive nature will never take us across the threshold into some new transcendental reality in which we come face to face with God.

However, if in the end mathematics is able to surmise all that exists in the physical universe, it will, at best, suggest a plan of 'how the universe functions' not '*why* it functions'. If, someday, it were found that the 'plan of God' is mathematical then God would simply have been located as a supreme designer; a somewhat agreeable position for many theologians, as it would, in their eyes, add weight to their conviction that God is real.

However, conjecture such as this is hardly a stable platform of absolute truth, or a reason to accept or reject a transcendental reality. I conclude that mathematics cannot add to, or subtract from, the proof of the existence of a transcendental reality. Mathematics is not sufficiently advanced for investigating any possible transcendental phenomenon.

We will now leave the world of mathematics and consider the elementary particles that make up our physical universe. Are there boundary fences around the behaviour of elementary particles, explained today in terms of the science of quantum mechanics? Does quantum mechanics allow us to realise the transcendental? Will the quanta point to the reality, or otherwise, of God?

2.3 The Quantum World

The dominant theory of creation, the 'Big Bang', suggests that elementary particles of nature, known as quarks, initially roamed freely in a sea of energy to become confined within neutrons and protons in well under a minute from the onset. During that first minute we are confidently told that the physical laws must have been changing. (Otherwise the theory of cosmic evolution does not hold up to scrutiny.) Finally, these universal laws settled to become those that are still prevalent today. Many fundamental mysteries remain, the most obvious being what the universe was like before it started expanding – before 'something' was there 'nothing'? Was there some form of 'potentiality'?

The 'ping-pong balls' of electrons that I was brought up with are now considered to be matter/energy consortiums with no fixed address – each one just a vague haze, often detected buzzing around an 'attractive' nucleus. They seem to be in several places at once. Is this latter image the reality of the fundamental building blocks of our universe? Or is our understanding of these elementary particles limited by our mental ability? For if we measure anything at all then the measurement can never be better than the ability of that measuring device. Imagine testing the effectiveness of a slimming diet by weighing oneself on a machine which normally weighed ocean-going ships to the nearest five tons – not much information about the reality of our weight there! Similarly our mind's 'blunt' imagination could well be the limiting factor when we try to discover the true nature of the elementary particles that make up our universe.

Today it is accepted that light is a particle and also a waveform – which leads to implications that are not always rational. Why do we need to use the analogies of particles and waveforms anyway? Reasons include the fact that, in general, the imagination of scientists, like all human imagination, is curtailed by objects and events that are familiar. So we use metaphor and analogies to help us understand and, from such concepts, scientists produce mathematical and other predictive models. Max Planck started all this in the early part of the twentieth century, when he defined a concept which later was used to analyse light. Light is not only wave-like, travelling as the waves on the sea, it is also considered as moving in discrete lumps, or quanta, the smallest of which is the photon.

Neither the wave nor the particle has to be true. Light may be of a form that does not have analogies in the world that we can perceive with our basic five senses. In fact we can never be sure just what light is, for we can only measure the effect that light has on other things. It is these observed effects that must be repeatable for science to accept a theory as being proven.

The nearer we get to dealing with the kind of objective measurement which is on the edge of mankind's knowledge, the more we become unsure of the mechanism which yields observable solutions.

There are today many theories that try to substantiate why quantum entities act as they do. There are suggestions that within each quanta there are 'strings' which have come together to produce 'superstrings' and these control the actions of the individual quanta. Scientific measurements indicate that quantum entities, such as light and electrons, travel as waves; even a single electron seems to spread out like the ripples on a pond. However, when an observation or measurement is made, the wave function collapses into a point-like particle.

The most amazing thing is that if, under certain conditions, a second electron is shot at the same target as a previous one (which has long since gone on its way), this second electron seems to know where the first one landed, and acts accordingly! Successive electrons will form a statistical pattern, which some eminent scientists interpret as requiring signals to travel backwards in time! All other interpretations, which can predict what will happen in quantum mechanics, appear to rely on separate particles having instantaneous communication between them, even when they are wide apart! This communication, being instantaneous, means that if speed is involved, it is infinite, and not limited by the speed of light, the theoretical maximum velocity of anything in our known universe!

Even if we know what happens under given conditions in the quantum world, the actual mechanism and how this mechanism operates, is still a mystery.

Why quantum theory works we simply do not know. We are like the driver of a car who has only been introduced to foot pedals and has no concept of the origin of the driving force, the engine. We do not know what we are controlling, only that it seems to work.

Once more a seemingly bottomless pit of unknown and changing rules and values – a far cry from a platform of absolute timeless truth. Perhaps the quantum world is an indicator that our physical world contains even more complex dimensions than time and space? Mark Hadley, writing in the *New Scientist* suggests that this quantum world could be inextricably linked to the cosmos in a form of 'space-time so dramatically warped that it bends back on itself like a knot.' One of my own conjectures is that there may be a commonality between the microscopic world of the quanta and the macroscopic world of the cosmos. It could be that in some unfathomable way every particle is actually connected to every other particle in the universe. This connection could be by something equivalent to an ideal, inelastic, solid 'rod' that nevertheless allows discrete movements. (Perhaps it is the weak force of gravity?) If one end of an ideal 'rod' is moved then instantaneously the whole universe becomes 'aware' of that movement and the whole system 'settles' into a new equilibrium, an unstable equilibrium, which causes further shifts and so on, each particle continually affecting all that exists.

In reality all our analysis of 'waveforms', 'lumps', 'rods' and so on is limited by our ability to imagine what is going on. We mostly succumb to descriptions that mirror known events or ideas derived from our everyday life. These descriptions, often in the form of metaphor, help scientists to relate to each other and progress their knowledge, perhaps in a similar way to the story-telling analogies so often found in world scriptures when there is an attempt to express the transcendental or to realise God. Typical of many analogies concerning the realisation of God is the one to be found in a Hindu scripture, *The Gospel of Ramakrishna*: 'There is oil in mustard seed, but one must press the seed to extract the oil...' This implies that one does not realise God without some effort on one's own part.

However, quantum mechanics will not in our present state of knowledge further our search for the truth of the transcendental. But the boundaries of our present quanta theories could point to a reality beyond our measuring instruments today which may have profound effects on many of our current theories, not least our understanding of the mind and consciousness. A point worth remembering when we are considering the possible immanence of God.

Well, no hard and fast conclusions concerning the reality of God so far, perhaps we will fare better by considering cosmology and creation.

2.4 Cosmology and Creation

All creation seems to be made of quanta 'stuff'. The twentieth-century astronomer Sir Arthur Stanley Eddington calculated the number of protons and electrons in the universe as approximately 2×10^{79}. (There have been other estimates, for example Andrei Linde writing in *Scientific American* suggests a figure of 10^{88} elementary particles.) However, even taking the former, this is a colossal number, two with 79 zeros behind it, reduces our common order of numbers to insignificance. For example if I had started counting on the 1st January 2000 and carried on for 1000 years, until 1st January 3000, at the rate of three counts per second, (with a day's break every leap year), I would count up to about 10,512,000,000. This is around 10 billion (10^{10}), which is 1 with 'only' ten zeros behind it.

Where then, did the universe come from? A difficult question, especially when one considers the immensity of the universe, e.g. 4,000 galaxies appear as but a grain of sand through the Hubble space telescope. Today there are many competing theories. I recollect many years ago being the guest of Professor Chandra Wickramasinghe at the Buddhist Centre at Taplow Court in Buckinghamshire and listening to a debate on the origin of the universe. They were discussing the most popular competing theories of the time, the 'Big Bang' versus the 'Steady State'. Both of these ideas have been with humanity for thousands of years as can be verified by reference to ancient world scriptures. The Steady State was recorded in Hindu and Buddhist literature in the form of cyclic or continuous evolution with spontaneous creation and annihilation always present within the universe, while the Big Bang is described in the book of Genesis (common to Jewish, Christian and Islamic beliefs) in the guise of a one-off, six-day creation. There are many more well-documented and succinctly argued theories derived from human observations; such as the 'Plasma Steady State' cosmology, or infinite universes found by theoretically traversing down black holes, or the 'Inflation Theory', which suggests that our complete universe is just 'one bubble' from an infinite set of bubbles. But invoking infinity, as we discussed in our search for God in the confines of mathematics, will give us any solution we care to name. Also, it is worth recalling that infinity has never been shown to actually exist in the physical universe.

Cosmological hypothesis and conjectures concerning the origin of our universe are far from being foolproof and are endlessly debated by scientists, all with their favourite theories. For example, the most popular *theory*, the Big Bang or 'Singularity', tells us that all we are able to see or measure in the universe is only a fraction (at the time of writing the estimates vary between 10 per cent and 25 per cent observable) of the amount, weight or mass required for the theory itself to be plausible at all. This is the 'missing mass' problem. Its current solution is to assume that there's a lot of 'cold dark matter' and 'hot dark matter' made from fundamental particles so far undetectable. This missing matter could account for the fact that the outer rims of galaxies appear to be rotating at the wrong speed. It seems that the only 'evidence' for dark matter is that, by assuming its existence, the cosmological theories work out right. A sceptic could conclude that the theory is up to 90 per cent in error at the present moment.

There are many other anomalies, such as explaining why the universe is so uniform on a large scale and at the same time contains the chaos that produces galaxies. With the great advances in terrestrial and geostationary telescopes today we can observe galaxies 15 billion light years away, yet on analysis they appear to be only two billion light years old. This may at first seem to be rational until we bring in another basic precept of scientific belief – that the speed of light in a vacuum is constant and finite, suggesting that the light from a galaxy 15 billion light years away will take 15 billion years to get here, i.e. there will be a delay of 15 billion years before we are aware of any event that took place at this enormous distance from us. How then can we observe a galaxy only two billion years old? Surely the light from it should take another 13 billion years to get here? Is it true or is it a fix to suggest, as most cosmologists do, that space acts like an elastic band so that one metre as measured on earth would have to take on a different length in space to allow this elaborate theory to hold together. This elastic measure makes concepts such as the 'Red Shift' make sense – these innovative ideas are essential to allow other philosophies, hypotheses, conjectures and theories to be valid.

And now we have eminent scientists such as Steven Chu of Stanford University suggesting that it is possible to measure wave packets that are faster than light. If this proposition is verified it would mean that many current theories would have to be drastically revised.

Is it beyond all doubt that our silent earth is spinning in a giant helical ellipse, pulled by an insignificant sun, in an insignificant galaxy? A galaxy whose sole object of existence seems to be to accelerate into an unknown void, or will it be eventually shown that we have replaced the ancient 'flat earth' myth with nothing more than a modern myth? No one knows the answer to such questions.

These fascinating evolving ideas about our universe, which include mind-bending concepts such as intelligent life forms on other planets, is not, for me, good enough to verify or dismiss the possibility of a transcendental reality. For even if we assume, for the moment, that the physics of the initial expansion caused by the Big Bang proves to have substance, maybe with the theory of countless 'superstrings' within each atomic particle, will it then give us the answer that there is no God? Most unlikely, for large galactic masses cannot congeal from a perfect expansion; it needs some perturbation from the onset. That is, the singularity must intrinsically contain chaos or randomness. Current theories of the initial expansion suggest that it is homogeneous, so why should randomness that is essential for matter to clump together, (forming galaxies, stars, planets, etc) exist? All randomness needs a defining system to produce it (e.g. random number generation). Randomness cannot 'just exist' on its own. Thus it appears that, to have randomness or chaos in the first place, we need an intelligence or a system to produce the right environment that will yield randomness. The most favoured system to account for the origin of our universe, the Big Bang, needs much further development indeed to prove that, unaided, phenomenal forces could emanate from within themselves. If the Big Bang suggests anything real at all, it suggests an intelligent starting point to our universe, which could well be a pointer to a transcendental truth and the reality of God.

I could go on theorising on the origin of the universe but, once again, it seems that our present knowledge is far from being conclusive. Sadly it seems that studying astronomy is not the absolute stable platform of truth, or bedrock. We humans seem to be more like newborn babies staring with fixed focus on an awesomeness, which we cannot really comprehend. What then is cosmology? It is interesting, fascinating, perhaps even useful, but it is certainly not an ultimate theory and unlikely ever to be such. It seems that here our knowledge may always be very much in flux. It was at Taplow Court that I finally concluded that even the most established theories in science are but vehicles on our journey of discovery. Vehicles become old, to be overtaken by new developments and we all quickly jump onto a more effective theory so that we can continue our captivating journey of worldly understanding.

Whatever fantastic future lies for humanity within the stars, I do not expect to see the actual 'face of God' by looking through a telescope!

The two areas of science that we have considered so far point towards intelligence and purpose within the creation of our universe and the human mind being limited, unable to fathom the 'spark' that makes it all happen. But disappointingly we are still left with the question of God's reality unanswered. Perhaps a consideration of the biological world will solve the riddle of whether God exists or not?

2.5 Genetics and the Origin of Life

June the 26th 2000 could well be the most remembered date of the third millennium. Why? Because it was on that day scientists announced that they had completed a draft of the human genome sequence. The human genome (the complete set of genes) is a genetic code that consists of only four chemical constituents (bases), yet it contains over three billion correctly sequenced parts, and if physically stretched out in a straight line it would be around two metres long. It exists in every living cell in our bodies and it is the key to all the biological attributes of our birth. Are we to believe that the totality of our humanity depends solely on this chemical, which has developed itself by random chance over billions of years, adapted by the blind selections of evolution? No of course not, for the totality of our humanity must at least include the way in which our brain becomes programmed by our surroundings from birth, and why should I assume that evolution is blind?

Charles Darwin at the end of the nineteenth century rationalised an amazingly powerful theory – life is an evolutionary process that biologically improves by a mechanism, which he called the 'Survival of the Fittest'. According to Darwin, all repetitions of significant patterns only emerge when a logical selection system (which is in itself a pattern), acts on them. This in turn is the idea of his natural selection, i.e. 'selection of the fittest' implies that something more suited (more intelligent maybe?) is doing the selection. This further implies that somehow, at the very *birth* of all evolutionary chains of events there is some form of intelligence or selection system that is *aware* of short significant patterns as they occur and holds onto them. A starting point is required, a chicken *or* an egg. Can such theories truly explain the complexities of nature that we observe today?

How, for example, does a 'blind' Darwinian explain, and more importantly prove, the fact that in some part of Thailand fireflies light up whole rows of trees with synchronised flashing – flashing in unison like gigantic Christmas trees, and what about the evolution of a butterfly, with its four distinct stages of egg, caterpillar, chrysalis and butterfly. In particular, how does he explain the evolutionary mechanism, which involves the caterpillar apparently 'liquefying' and then reconstituting itself as a butterfly, all the while being encapsulated within its chrysalis shell?

Then again, consider our human form of reproduction. Natural enough, you might say. Evolutionists may try and tell us that it is nothing but the result of millions of people with no sexual drive randomly jiggling about and happening to copulate successfully. Or is it that our urge to reproduce is due to an inner drive already built into us all? I don't know how it is for you, but personally I am part of the latter group. Could it be that those who truly believe in blind evolution are part of the former group?

It seems that far from being blind, evolution has in-built tendencies, just as reproduction, survival, etc, is already built into every living thing. We are all part of 'the unbroken chain of life'.

Reflexes give us an overwhelming desire to procreate – or at least take part in its initial stages. This naturally leads us to ask questions such as, 'Where does this motivation to breed come from?' Or in the broadest concept, 'Where does motivation itself come from?' The fact that in some instances (e.g. electromagnetic attraction) we can measure a force of attraction, or motivation, makes some scientists suggest that it 'just happens' – like ostriches with their heads in the sand they refuse to consider any possible broader reality that may exist.

If we take the absolutists application of Darwin's selection of the fittest concepts we find that initially our ancestors could have been 'simple-minded' amino acids; or even molecules which became more complex by joining together, perhaps within a soup of rock minerals or clay deposits. In other words these 'amino acid ancestors' of ours must have been indulging in the fun of pouncing on other comely amino acids to produce more complex offspring.

It follows that the motivation of our amino acids must have started when they were mere atoms electromagnetically attracted to other nearby atoms. To put our 'atom ancestors' into human terms, they were seeking to experience the ecstasy of being in contact with another atom and becoming a simple molecule. But, wait, what about the basic 'particle' or quark? To become an atom it apparently longed to be absorbed into, or united with, other subatomic 'things' to become its dream piece of matter? Go down past the radiation blips and postulate the magic of strings, whose only desire in life is to become a superstring, and so on and so on. No matter how 'simple' you assume the form of our first ancestor, the inner urge to combine and become more complex seems to be always present.

I realise that I have greatly over-simplified some current theory, nevertheless the message is clear: it is far more logical to assume that motivation is part and parcel of existence itself, than to assume that the motivation to breed suddenly occurred.

So, it seems that we are left with the questions: 'Where does all this motivation to join together come from? Why should 'motivation' itself exist at all?'

Genes are not, as some would have us believe, the prime movers of life. They are merely at an arbitrary point on the spectrum of 'cooperation'. In the struggle to exist it may be an atom or a superstring that is behind 'it all happening'. An atomic particle such as a proton or an electron is far more permanent than a gene.

Of course, the level of the gene is important to us for it contains information about our biological make-up at a level with which we can easily relate. However, just as the light switch does not tell us why the light goes on and off (let alone who installed the light in the first place), so studying the gene is intrinsically a limited vehicle that is most unlikely to reveal the secrets of our own personal existence or our complex human consciousness.

Today's evolving concepts of biology, especially genetics, are some of the most rapidly advancing fields of science today. Understandably, many people believe that they will give ultimate answers. But by their very nature, they are limited to our worldly, mortal existence. Genetics and the study of biology enhance the details of ancient Chinese knowledge that appreciated that there are patterns to life itself. Thus I cannot use this branch of science if I am to grasp any deeper meaning for my own life, my individuality, my *being* itself.

In the case of evolution, even if we demonstrate spontaneous and evolving life in a laboratory, we are the designers, the partakers and the observers of the experimental, and from quantum mechanics, it has been a long-established fact that simply by observing an action we affect that action! The setting up of a system *in itself* makes a great deal of difference to the outcome of the experiment; it cannot represent the mindless form of evolution that some are trying to verify. By bringing the right conditions together, scientists are the creators of the evolving life forms that they are trying to demonstrate are spontaneous. All demonstrations intrinsically need starting conditions; they have to be set up. It is impossible to demonstrate undirected spontaneity. For example, starting with our planet earth, the logic goes something like this:

Q What would naturally set up the right system for evolution of life on this planet?

A Why, another system, for example, the solar system.

Q And what would naturally set up the right system for the solar system to evolve?

A Probably a galaxy.

Q And what would set up the right system for a galaxy to evolve?

And so on and so on. Each time a system needs a system or a set of rules to bring it into existence. Life requires direction. No system that mankind has ever envisaged has ever arisen spontaneously.

Although it may prove to be true that life is formed through 'self-assembly', I believe that we are chasing the rainbow's end when we assert that one day we will prove that the complete system of evolution is simply 'self-created'. For 'self-assembly' is only an automatic process set in train by an intelligent agent, whereas 'self-created' implies no intelligent input whatsoever. No reality that science has ever evaluated points to such a strange proposal as 'self-creation'. It is only to be found in the creative imagination of some scientists.

There are today computer software programs that mimic evolution. It is suggested that these intelligently designed, purpose-built, computer programs (based upon, say, a Mandlebrot set), show how extrapolations from simple amino acids could have produced the complexities of metamorphic life. But such interesting, contrived illustrations are no more proof of 'natural' evolution than the drawing of angels proves that angels exist.

Stuart Kauffman suggests that, 'Biological evolution may have been shaped by more than just natural selection. Computer models suggest that certain complex systems tend towards self-organisation.' Self-organisation suggests that motivation is already built into our biological world. There are advocates against finding reality in computer models. John Maynard Smith of the University of Sussex, who pioneered the use of mathematics in biology, has concluded that artificial life (computer software) is 'basically a fact-free science.' Staggering, unverifiable claims of biologists are not new and remind me more of the nineteenth-century scientists who 'proved' that life occurred spontaneously in a sealed glass jar. In reality the essence of life was contained in life forms finer than they could observe at the time with the instruments available. Their faith in the universality of their ideas was more in keeping with fundamentalists proclaiming their religious beliefs than scientists dealing with facts.

Blind, undirected evolution theory is intrinsically unprovable; nevertheless a form of *purposeful* evolution (even in its apparent randomised form) happens to be the most agreeable possibility to me at the moment. It could well be the natural progression from an intelligent first position.

There is no doubt that genetics has today mutated from a science to a dangerous practical engineering form. The genetic engineering of the future could affect every child that is born. Genes may be checked and decisions made on whether the child will be born at all, by using the option of simply killing the defective child in the womb at a premature state. Some societies allow termination of the embryonic foetus, for many reasons, including suspected Down's Syndrome. Perhaps abortion-on-demand will eventually become acceptable for details such as the position of a beauty spot? All parents seem to crave 'perfection' but should they be the arbiters of future human life?

The rules and ethics of genetics are at the moment like a quicksand.

What, for example, if a sheep embryo was genetically modified, replaced in the womb of a ewe so that a human baby resulted? Would the offspring be human, with all the rights and privileges implied? Perhaps the newborn would have the brain and torso of a human, communicate and show the love and compassion of a human, but physically still be made up of lamb chops, ram's horns and cloven feet! In such a case questions of ethics would be truly mind-blowing.

Genetics, like atomic power and industrial pollution, could well affect every future living soul, perhaps offering a cure for the 'disease' of ageing. Our understanding of genetics is changing rapidly at present. Eventually, I suspect, it will settle down and take its place as another of mankind's great discoveries from an infinite pool of *that which already exists*.

Where is all this leading in terms of ultimate truth? Sadly, I feel, in the wrong direction. A direction where we cannot even begin to answer questions such as: 'Why motivation?' 'Why should there be any desire on the part of strings, quarks and the like to react together (primitive copulation?) in the first place?' 'From where does this seemingly intrinsic form of motivation or purpose arise?'

Perhaps, many thousands of years ago, the writers of that part of the biblical Apocrypha known as Ecclesiasticus, had more knowledge than some credit them with, especially when one considers that in the very first chapter it is written,

All wisdom is from the Lord; she dwells with him for ever. Who can count the sands of the sea, the raindrops, or the days of unending time? Who can measure the height of the sky, the breadth of the earth, or the depth of the abyss? Wisdom was first of all created things; **intelligent purpose has existed from the beginning***.*

To return to the core question, does our knowledge of biology in any way eliminate the reality of God? The simple answer is 'definitely not!' It could eventually be seen to be as the American

President, Bill Clinton, suggested when the announcement that the 3.1 billion sub-units of human DNA, the human genome, had been decoded, 'Today we are learning the language in which God created life.'

Genetics and the origin-of-life theories have given us no firm facts to date concerning the reality, or otherwise, of an overall intelligence, or God. The theory of evolution is a wonderful vehicle, it illuminates so much, but to suggest that evolution is blind is a sign of human conceit, not a sign of any reality. We may be discovering how to assemble the jigsaw of our existence, but it is good to remember that even jigsaws were produced by an intelligent agent.

It is now time to move on to the last subject of science we are to consider, human communication and information itself.

2.6 Information Technology

The mythical 'cyberspace brain' is nowhere, yet accessible every-where. This is the might of the portable telephone when connected to the super-powerful Internet and World Wide Web.

Due to the unprecedented rate of advancement in the field of electronics and its supportive technologies the whole world is experiencing the birth pangs of global communication and information technology (IT). This is a revolution that is expected to have more impact on the lifestyle of everyone than did the Agricultural or the Industrial Revolutions.

Mass communication may turn out to be the greatest gift so far for the human race, for it may become impossible for power-hungry leaders to dupe masses when each one of us has free access to a worldwide information network. IT could break down ancient prejudice allowing human compassion to flood across the barriers of race, religion and nationalism. Or it could simply herald the ultimate, unfettered supply and demand cycle, the final marketplace, the triumph of consumerism. Will it increase each human being's freedom or will we all be reduced to being part of a cyber-network; a mere neuron in a super brain?

These questions are for the future to answer, but for now we could ask if there are any intrinsic limits to our accumulation of knowledge, and what is known about information itself.

There is a growing band of physicists who are putting forward a notion that the information within intelligent communication is a super-weird new substance, more ethereal than matter or energy, but every bit as real and perhaps even more fundamental. They are suggesting that information is a kind of subtle substance that lies behind and beneath the physical stuff. It is this that allows 'entanglement', whereby, according to Charles Bennett of IBM Research, 'Distant particles are linked in a way that they classically couldn't be unless they were in the same place.' Perhaps the quantum landscape is the way it is because it conforms to the laws that rule some deeper level where information is supreme.

The communication of intelligent information could turn out to be our guide to a fuller understanding of the cosmos. There are inexplicable amounts of energy in, for example, cosmic and gamma rays, which bombard our planet. Some of the energy sources for this bombardment have been estimated to emit, in seconds or at most in minutes, more energy than the sun will in its entire lifetime – currently predicted to be some ten billion years. Theoretically this energy could contain within it a form of 'universal communication' from some super-intelligence.

Or consider the 'background noise', thought to be the remnants of the cosmic Big Bang. It is like a giant's hiss that is echoing around the galactic system. Conceivably, this 'background noise' could be the most efficient way of transmitting information between intelligent forces within our universe. For after all if we observe the most sophisticated form of compressed information transmission, it would appear to be very similar to that giant's hiss, the hiss of white noise.

The human race seems to be hell-bent on trying to obtain all the possible information that exists in the universe. Is this information, in itself, finite and fixed or is it infinite, never-ending? This is a difficult, but answerable question. In the first place, as we saw earlier when we looked at the boundaries of mathematics, the real world does not contain anything that is actually infinite. Yes, things can be very large indeed but they are still finite, like the number of particles estimated to be in our universe. Infinity is a brilliant mathematical tool, but it has never been found to exist in the real world or universe. Thus infinity is a theory, a conjecture, a 'fix', that allows mathematics to predict reality – it is not how the universe itself is – just as a tool for digging the garden is not the garden itself.

If we randomly press the keys of a word processor for ever (infinity) then eventually we could find a sequence of letters and spaces in the correct order for all that has ever been written by the human race to date. Now consider the practical case. How long do you imagine it would take one million random typists using a million active word processors, to produce the simple sequential information in the sentence, 'The quick brown fox jumps over the lazy dog'?

Let's work it out by first assuming what we 'know' about our *actual* universe:

- Starting at the beginning of time – at the assumed origin of our universe, taking, for simplicity, the age of our universe to be limited by the Hubble constant estimated to be between 12 and 18 billion years.
- There are 50 possible characters on each word processor (ignoring the complexity of having to use the shift key to obtain upper case etc).
- Our random typists all type away continuously for 24 hours a day at the rate of one character per second.
- There is no external intelligent agent selecting, and holding on to, any correct individual letter as it appears.

Now there is a 50 to one chance of the first letter 't', as in 'the', being correctly chosen, i.e. on average the word processor keys will have to be pressed 50 times to get the first letter 't'. To get the second letter, 'h', correctly following the first will, on average, take another 50 presses. So to obtain 'th' in the correct sequence without intelligent interference will take on average 50 times 50 presses. Thus to find 'the' correctly sequenced it will require, on average,

50 times 50 times 50 (50^3) presses of the keyboard. Or for 'n' correct letters and spaces it will require 50^n presses of the keyboard. Now just how many possible key presses could be achieved if it were possible to start at the estimated beginning of the universe? It would take the number of years in seconds, times the number of word processors that were continuously used, which by straightforward multiplication using the information above, gives an approximate 5.68×10^{17} as a maximum number of key depressions that could have occurred.

Thus, the maximum number of words and spaces we could, on average, correctly obtain, 'n', in 18 billion years can be found when $50^n = 5.68 \times 10^{17}$.

Given n = log 5.68×10^{17}/ log 50 makes the maximum number of correctly sequenced letters or spaces ('n') approximately 10.

This means that by today, statistically speaking, only one of the word processors will have managed to correctly produce not even the full sentence 'the quick brown fox jumps over the lazy dog' but merely 'the quick'. It seems that a real number of random typists, in a real universe, would fall far short of producing even the complete works of Shakespeare, let alone the complete writing of the human race to date.

Why then, is information so abundant? Surely we have a limited universe (maximum current estimates being 10^{88} elementary particles)? Are we not dealing with limited information? Perhaps not. For one thing information is much more complex than the addition of atoms. For example, as previously mentioned, it only takes four different substances (nucleotides) to produce the human genome.

When I was first told that the number of paths or connections between the brain cells of each individual human being exceeds the number of atoms in the universe I found it very hard to believe.

But it is true. Furthermore, the number of possible combinations of our neurons far exceeds the total paths. But the real world is even more complex as we live in 'time' and this produces sequences of patterns that are vastly larger, numerically, than the number of possible combinations.

It is sequences and patterns we are mostly aware of. The hypnotic effect of acquiring information is awesome. My optician, Patrick Round, tells me most people have the ability to distinguish about 16 million different colours, while Mike Creese of HTV Studios in Cardiff assures me that today a typical colour TV has over 140 stripes per line. Putting these two simple facts together was quite a sobering thought. It turns out that, if all humanity spent their complete lives staring at a TV screen, far from seeing all there is to see, our combined viewing would not even approach viewing all the possible coloured patterns of just the first line of one frame of a 625-line TV. In fact not even all the elementary particles in the universe could *discretely* store *all* the possible coloured patterns that could be generated by that first line (i.e. 10^{88} is vastly less than the colossal number represented by $(16 \times 10^6)^{140}$, or 3.8×10^{1008}, where 16 million is a typical figure for the number of colours that an average human eye can resolve and 140 is the number of coloured stripes in one line of one frame of a TV picture). Even if we could limit the colours to say, ten, we still would fall far short of all the combinations of the first line of a TV picture! (10^{88} combinations is many orders smaller than 10^{141}).

Information technology, by its very nature, will only disclose to each one of us a minuscule amount of all the possible information that the universe can generate. Even allowing for the most sophisticated form of data compression techniques or hierarchy grouping formats feasible it would still be impossible to store all the information generated by the universe using the finite number of fundamental particles in the universe itself. It appears at present that IT has opened up a Pandora's box filled with countless bits of interconnected information. Whatever the truth turns out to be concerning the communication of information, to date it has yielded no clues as to the reality or otherwise of God. Information itself is, unfortunately, just another limited concept.

Having sufficient knowledge of relevant information can certainly help us to have some 'power' over our environment. But an overload of knowledge simply results in the mind itself being caught in the 'web of information'. Trying to cope with unlimited information dims the transcendental reality that a clear mind can experience. When it comes to realising God, this worldly information 'dumbs down' rather than 'lights up' our path.

The colossal information in our universe is limited, but compared with our finite lifetime it is more than sufficient to clog the mind. The vastness of possible information for our minds to absorb more than reinforces Isaac Newton's claim that his lifetime's work was the observation of but one pebble on the beach of eternity. My quest is not the analysis of the pebbles, but the beach itself. Experiencing the reality of a beach is dramatically beyond experiencing and knowing all the properties of a pebble. The possibility of the transcendental, God, is not confined within the 'information pebble', no matter how complex that pebble might be.

So I conclude that the vastness of information, powerful as it may be, does not in itself give us proof for or against the reality of God, although such considerations will probably enhance our understanding of the attributes of God, providing we can first establish that God exists.

2.7 Seeking the Source

A web of information, in which most of us become entangled, sur-rounds us. This web may well be preventing the possibility of us acquiring transcendental sight. We become entangled with smart computer programs that seem at first sight to suggest that intelligence is not required to be behind the existence of our universe. Yet even the most outstanding simulation of evolution cannot work without 'intelligent' selection of the best outcome at each stage.

Appreciation of art and music is beyond science. For example, if I set up a laboratory taking all the ingredients that produced Vincent Van Gogh's painting of *Chair with Pipe*, I would never produce an identical picture. In a very limited way the pictures of, say, Van Gogh may be thought to be like transcendental information, in as much as they cannot be produced by experimentation.

Human understanding encompasses such things as beauty and form, a much broader reality than science alone. Why, for instance, should I find snow-capped mountain peaks so awesome and beckoning when exploring such an alien environment for our ancestors would herald danger, suffering and death?

Conventional science, by its very nature, limits our understanding to a general, repeatable, non-personal reality, whereas if the transcendental exists I have a strong suspicion that it will normally be realised by unique individual events. Like seeing a kingfisher once and once only, I cannot repeat this experience at will, just to satisfy other people's lack of belief.

It is interesting to observe people who rummage around on the frontiers of science and mathematics reverting to artistic or 'sacred' metaphor as they struggle to grapple with the awesomeness of what is being uncovered. And this awe often appears to enlarge their own ego, which traps them into believing that nothing could possibly exist beyond the worldly logic of conventional scientific method. They become bound by the information that they are uncovering. It reminds me of when, as a child, I caught my first tadpole. In my excitement I was overawed by it all.

There are many fascinating theories that attempt to logically suggest that intelligence never has been necessary for evolution to occur. One of the more elegant explanations for the amazing structural properties of inorganic and organic entities was clearly given by Donald E Ingber when he wrote in January 1998 *Scientific American*:

An astoundingly wide variety of natural systems, including carbon atoms, water molecules, proteins, viruses, cells, tissues and even humans and other living creatures, are constructed using a common form of architecture known as **tensegrity***. The term refers to a system that stabilises itself mechanically because of the way in which tensional and compressive forces are distributed and balanced within the structure.*

Ingber further explains that such cells produce proteins which self-assemble forming a matrix of anchoring scaffolds which can give rise to complex organisms. Thus without any external help complex things form from their own inherent structure. But, is it all so 'simple'? How, for example, can the 254 or so distinct cell types in the human body evolve by cooperation on a grand structural scale when they can only exist in the first place if held within an external structure. No doubt I could, as I am sure you could, think up ways that this could possibly have happened; such as the theory based upon 'attractors' and 'repellers' as defined by Jack Cohen and Ian Stuart in their book, *The Collapse of Chaos*. They assert that a dynamical system tends naturally towards an attractor in the form of a loop so that, 'If some disturbance from outside the dynamical system drives the point off the loop, the spiral motion pushes it back again...' But do these ideas truly begin to explain unintelligent evolution? They are more akin to the mind's artistic flair dreaming up an explanation in keeping with a theory that one is trying to verify in the first place. Then again we have John Horgan writing concerning 'the edge of chaos' on behalf of the Santa Fe Institute and explaining a very plausible concept for biological evolution:

Nothing novel can emerge from systems with high degrees of order and stability, such as crystals. On the other hand, completely chaotic systems, such as turbulent fluids or heated gases, are too formless. Truly complex things – amoebae, 'bond traders' and the like – appear at the border between rigid order and randomness.

An appealing hypothesis, but one which does little to explain the underlying motivation behind evolution.

In this chapter we have seen that mathematics, science and technology are seeking ultimate truth, unfolding the jigsaw of our environment and our biological make-up. Due to the complexity of our universe, this appears to be an intriguing, never-ending journey of discovery. But, when all is said and done, they are tools that evaluate reality using worldly wisdom only. Worldly wisdom, although it can bring about profound benefits, is by its very nature limited.

When I was a child I often played on the grassy banks of the village pond. There was a large pipe to take away surplus water, but as a child I believed that it was 'just there' of its own accord. In my undeveloped mind no one had been responsible for its installation.

In the same way some claim that 'blind' evolution exists. Evolution is a theory, a supreme vehicle with which to explore our physical and biological history. To suggest that it is anything more than a theory limits the full potential of our humanity being realised. Believing in 'blind' evolution can fool us into 'drawing the line of meaning' of our lives well before we have explored its fulness.

Are we to believe that, although each of us are living entities of unfathomable complexity developed over countless millions of years, biological life has never required any form of intelligent guidance or 'Supreme Being'. While, on the other hand, a most elementary burst of 'Morse-coded' signal emanating from space would herald a plethora of human belief systems based upon an *intelligent* source of that signal.

Although we have not yet verified or dismissed the reality of God, five points have arisen, which indicate the possibility of an intelligent input to our existence. These are:

1. Quantum mechanics and communication theories indicate that there is more built into matter itself than simply mass, energy and a sense of time.
2. For a system to evolve there needs to be a second system to contain it; and that second system must itself be embraced within a third system and so on – possibly indicating an intelligent starting point beyond our space, energy and time-dependent world.
3. 'Motivation' or 'purpose' seems to be intrinsic within all things.
4. All knowledge, whether scientific or religious, is arrived at through experience. It is our confidence that increases by having similar, or repeated, experiences or by other people we trust telling us of their experiences.
5. Science is uncovering a jigsaw of information that already exists in one form or another.

Perhaps it was the exciting, childlike predictions found in science and mathematics that fired my imagination and led me to become a professional engineering scientist where I have tried to take on board the findings of people like the founder of the science of magnetism, William Gilbert. He suggested, in 1600, 'Let whosoever would make the same experiments handle the bodies not heedlessly and clumsily but carefully, skilfully and deftly.' Science, like all human knowledge, is a minefield and, if Gilbert was right when he pleaded for us to handle bodies...carefully, skilfully and deftly, how much more careful must we be when we attempt an experiment to find out if the transcendental actually exists.

Mathematics, science and technology are in some respects like a bunch of beautiful fibre optic 'straws' waving to and fro, with little lights at the end of each one nodding and bowing like ripe corn – each light emanating from a common source, the one great source. In this analogy, the tools of science are at best only able to analyse the properties of the fibre itself, not the light that they contain – the force within the fibre. Every little light transcends the medium (fibre optic) which contains it, and it becomes more and more obvious that, metaphorically, mathematics, science and technology only measure the properties of the fibre. They are all but tools limited to the observation, study and modification of our worldly environment.

I am seeking to experience the source - the great light itself.

Chapter 3

Approaching God

*This chapter sets out to establish **bedrock** so that a path to the transcendental can be realised.*

3.1 Origins

One skewed footprint in the fossilised volcanic ash of northern Tanzania indicates that early man turned and looked behind him.

Something must have crossed his mind, a thought which caused him to turn, on that day, over three and a half million years ago. Was it a simple animal-like thought? A thought perhaps induced by the dread of being pursued by a predator? Or was it a more human, contemplative or reflective thought? Today we still have the unhurried spore of that man. I wonder if we still have the remnants of his god?

Most people alive today believe in God. Even in apparently secular societies like Britain at least 60 per cent, and some say over 95 per cent, of the population believe that there is some form of god.

From where does the concept of God arise? Why should God be necessary at all? Is God simply a figment of human imagination?

When contemplating such questions it is tempting to agree with someone like the British astronomer, Patrick Moore. He and I were in Bournemouth in the summer of 1989, at an international microchip design meeting. Patrick had been the guest speaker and I the chairman. In the bar afterwards, I asked him if he believed in

God. 'These things are unanswerable – and thus a waste of time,' was his breathless, staccato reply.

His remark momentarily choked the conversation, and scattered my thoughts. Why was it that I could organise grand conferences for hundreds of top industrial and academic professionals concerned with one of the most advanced technologies ever encountered and yet, with scant exception, I could not even begin to discuss my absolute belief in a transcendental God?

For me, God encompasses yet exceeds that which can be explained by or within the phenomenal or physical universe itself.

There are many human conjectures concerning God that may or may not be a true reflection of the reality of God; this I term the 'god phenomenon'. The 'god phenomenon' is all human concepts, beliefs and understandings that point to God. The god phenomenon is the total human understanding and action under the generic term 'God', and includes all forms of speculation from crystals and natural objects, ancestral worship, mysticism and reincarnation to the personal Creator, Nirvana and the 'Greater Consciousness' along with all forms of ritual, culture and belief. Thus God is the reality that we are aiming to distil from the human understanding which is the god phenomenon. The god phenomenon may or may not contain information concerning the reality that is God.

I believe that a deep understanding of the boundless God first came to me in the early 1940s when I was just three years old, but it was not until the spring of 1990 that I felt the need to explore the ramifications of that experience in depth and with rigour. I needed to seek out and try to express a little more of this 'other' dimension that I had been aware of for so long. For it was a dimension of my life that I had rarely acknowledged.

It came to me that my best start was to read contemplatively the sacred scriptures of the world's faiths. By sacred scripture I mean writings that are revered by large numbers of people who believe that these contain absolute truths of, and that they come from, God.

My reading soon progressed to lengthy discussions with adherents of many different faiths. I was not simply seeking a critical exercise for my mind and intellect; I was looking for a spiritual experience, which I hoped would lead to a deeper understanding of the god phenomenon.

One of the many people I have had the privilege of in-depth discussions with is one of the older statesmen of religion, Victor Steele. Victor is infused with broad-based biblical knowledge, powerful moral beliefs and true altruistic love. He is a 'pillar' of Llandaff Cathedral. I recall mentioning to Victor that I longed to show that there is a bedrock of absolute truth for the existence of God. To this he replied, 'Many have tried this from different points of view. You are too idealistic; for God is beyond all proof...the best that we will ever achieve is faith.'

I could identify with these words. Yet surely some form of 'proof' must have been available to everyone who has faith? Even if the proof is only that they cannot think of any other alternative. Seeking a 'proof' for the existence of God is not necessarily like 'testing' God by looking for miracle cures or throwing myself out of a tenth-storey window expecting God to catch me. I was convinced that there was a proof, even if it was far more difficult than any that I have ever attempted to establish as a professional engineer.

There are many dimensions to life, and for me the ancient Indian scriptures, the *Bhagavad-Gita*, puts the human condition very succinctly by suggesting that there are five different dimensions or levels that we encounter in our human condition. It tells us that, 'Our basic animal senses are superior to simple matter; the mind is higher than our senses; intelligence is still higher than the mind; and the soul, or spirit, is even higher than the intelligence.' We are seeking to uncover as much as possible of the truth concerning the spiritual dimension of humankind.

I have spent much of my lifetime in the fascinating yet frustrating occupation of listening to academics, theologians, agnostics, atheists, humanists and others who claim to know this truth. There are people who are out to prove or disprove the reality of God through logic, science, mathematics, scriptural texts, miracles, prophecy, paranormal events, UFOs, extra-terrestrial life forms and so on. The list is endless. With such a plethora of information I will have to be very careful how I choose the path so that I do not get bogged down under those mountains of 'information' discussed in the last chapter.

In traditional science, if one is trying to verify and explore a subject, it is essential to start with known facts and observations. This is because all things are relative, so if we find an absolute truth, we can compare our other findings with this truth. Everything that we are familiar with is related in some way to everything else. To investigate the reality of God we must have a foundation of absolute truth. For without a stable platform of truth, everything that we measure would be distorted by the inaccuracies built in from the start.

As an engineering scientist I believe in an orderly and systematic progress, starting from such a known point, and with a clearly defined destination. To substantiate any claim that 'God is a reality', requires a true basis, or bedrock, from which such a claim can be evaluated. Archimedes, when explaining the power of a lever, had it right when he said, 'Give me but one firm spot on which to stand and I will move the earth.'

What then can be the firm spot for evaluating the reality, or otherwise, of the transcendental God? Where will I find a platform of unchanging truth about God?

I have always found this an intriguing, and at the same time a very vexing, question, one which has led me to ask myself what could have caused mankind to know God or to postulate gods in the first place?

When I initially pondered on the origin of the god phenomenon the problem seemed to be more a jungle of possibilities than anything susceptible to simple logical analysis. I was aware that other people were at different levels of understanding and personal development. Many people seemed to have become entrapped, fixed in an attitude regarding the origin, reality and 'characteristics' of God, holding unyielding convictions in the teeth of all contrary evidence. There seemed to be an infinite number of possibilities.

Fortunately, through study, meditation and prayer, the jungle thinned and I found that I could encompass the most significant possibilities for the origin of the god phenomenon into just three categories.

Firstly, we could put it down to a form of human development or evolution. An imaginary god could have been conjured up to explain collective ignorance and later have been spiced with human artistic imagination. This I call the 'Evolutionary God'.

Secondly, it could be that God is a reality. The revelations that have come to us ostensibly from God, through prophets, seers, gurus and the like could bear true witness to the reality of God. That is, reality expounded and verified through scripture. I will refer to this category as the 'Scriptural God'.

Third and last, the origin of the god phenomenon may be found in our own inner world; a world we could think of as intuitive awareness; a result of private inner recognition, separate from any learned reaction. This I term the 'Inner God'.

In practice the picture is complex. Features of all three categories are impressed upon our character through the social environment in which we find ourselves, while our actual beliefs are determined by inborn components of our personality, which in turn determine our logical or emotional reactions. If our conclusions are to have value, we must ensure that we do not miss the obvious, so let us briefly explore some initial thoughts and discoveries concerning the possible origin of transcendental thought. We will restrict these initial investigations to the three basic categories outlined above before we attempt too many layers of complexity.

3.2 Evolutionary Limits

The suggestion that God is 'confined to the mind of humankind' is considered by some to be supported by evolutionary theories. Such theories suggest that God is not real at all, but merely a figment of human imagination. So we'll make a start by considering possible historical evidence for and against the reality of God.

For our ancient ancestors, knowledge of parents and grandparents may have been sufficient. Stories of their own ancestors, their past exploits and their epoch-making travels may have been satisfactory for a while, then questions beyond known ancestors would have been asked. The 'Adam and Eve' of so many world myths would be born.

Then would have come the inevitable, 'Who produced Adam and Eve?' And the quest for the originator of all things would have had its start. A creator would have to have some shape or form to be understandable. This is where human, and even animal, characteristics could well have been grafted onto an early concept of God.

As the millennia rolled by, the god phenomenon could have taken on the many forms that we are familiar with today.

The Greeks had their gods of war and love. It was claimed that some of the Greek gods were actually born on this earth, like the god Hermes who is purported to have first come into the world as a baby in a cave high up the mountain of Zirin on the Peloponnese peninsula.

Some thousands of years earlier the people of the Indian subcontinent spoke of gods who were part animal yet human, while the 'One God' concept, derived from the many springs and tributaries of countless centuries, became a deep river of belief for Aryans in the ancient Babylonian Empire. This belief caused the Pharaoh Akhenaten to abandon Egyptian polytheism and its chief god Amun in the fourteenth century BCE, and to build the great city of Akhetaten – 'the place of the origin of the Sun Disk', the Aten. The 'One God' doctrine arising from the Zoroastrian beliefs reverberated with the Hebrews, who successfully championed the concept of only one God – successfully, for today it is a mainstream belief of countless religions.

Life and its origins are among the great unknowns. Death is another.

Scattered all over western Europe are the burial chambers containing the bones of ancient Celtic leaders from five hundred generations ago, suggesting that mankind anticipated that there was more to his existence than simply biological life. The practice of constructing burial mounds containing artefacts with dead bodies reached its zenith in the magnificent Egyptian pyramids, which contained glittering treasures for the rebirth of their dead and mummified nobility. China's great dynasties, whose leaders craved immortality, constructed for themselves huge chambers for their full-sized armies of protective terracotta soldiers. Building these great mausoleums took great wealth, organisation, perseverance and a tremendous leap of imagination; for surely all who have seen the dead body of a loved one must realise that physical death is final?

I was with my own father when he died at the grand old age of 91. I heard his last breath; I felt his last heartbeat. His death, like all deaths, was absolute. Death is not just another illness, for not to have biological life or consciousness in any form that we know, is seemingly the end. For so many, it is an unwanted and incomprehensible end. Moreover, in the minds of men – through memory, dreams and induced dream states – the dead live on. It is not unreasonable to suppose that a conflation of desire and human imagination gave rise to the concept of after-life, which in turn induced beliefs concerning the reality of God.

We may ask ourselves, still pursuing the evolutionary strand, if God is after all only an addition to ritual. The ritual that is associated with our desire to improve our chances of survival. Peering into mankind's prehistory could throw some light on this subject. There are many views concerning the date of the first *Homo sapiens*. These vary from the few thousand years suggested by ancient written material, to millions of years as indicated by fossil remains.

There are even suggestions that humanity commenced countless aeons ago elsewhere in the cosmos. The work by some astronomers, such as Fred Hoyle, has led some to conclude that life commenced in gigantic intergalactic clouds, while others suggest that there is evidence that, for countless millennia, space vehicles landed on earth from unknown origins in deep space, bringing with them the DNA for human existence.

Of all possibilities, the most widely accepted at present is the assumption that mankind evolved here on earth from a common animal ancestor. The pattern suggested by K P Oakley is typical. He has estimated that the earliest primate stage of emergence took place some 70 million years ago, incipient hominids about 12 million years ago and the oldest tool-making hominoids about one million years ago. Fossil remains are, in our present era, very scanty, ensuring that the actual date estimates are in a continuous state of flux. Nevertheless they indicate the order of time that we are discussing at the moment.

We could speculate that primitive people, many hundreds of thousands of years ago, realised the significance of the patterns of nature. These patterns would have been vital, especially to the tribes who, we are currently told, moved north out of Africa. Some of these tribes eventually occupied the fertile wooded valleys of southern Europe. Initially they would have been overjoyed at being able to predict the animal migration patterns. As the years went by it would have become obvious that there were important variations from year to year. Their sense of helplessness in the face of these variations may have been ameliorated by simple social acts – such as in the telling of folk tales and illustrating them in mime. When patterns were discerned which appeared to relate abundance with human movements, words or song, the dawn of human ritual would have arrived.

These rituals could have heralded more sophisticated and complex acts, such as the making of simple models, and painting images of the animals – the sort of thing that my wife, Jeanette, and I first experienced when visiting prehistoric cave paintings of the Perigord in France, back in 1982. Just outside Les Eyzies and in other lesser-known caves we saw for ourselves the Upper Palaeolithic art – which is estimated to be some 17 to 24 thousand years old.

Horses, bison, deer and other animals had been captured deep in the caves. Captured, that is, by coloured pigments smeared and blown onto the rocks by the light of rudimentary oil lamps, thousands of years before our visit. You could feel that somehow the people who practised this primitive art form had held the animals' essence, or soul, in the caves. The artists were strangers to us. They would never know of our existence, yet through their art we were aware of them, and the beauty of their art seemed to be still calling out to the animals to return each year.

These wonderful cave paintings in the southern parts of Europe are not unique; they are among the many thousands of others found from Asia to North Africa. Worldwide petrograms, or rock paintings, of New Stone Age Neolithic man supplement these underground paintings. Petrograms are still produced by the Aboriginal people of Australia today. These great works of art all bear witness to mankind's imaginative powers and could be examples of their beliefs.

Then must have come the discovery that seeds from the winter store actually grew into edible things. Planting and harvesting would have formed an elementary form of farming even when families moved seasonally, and soothsayers who could say when to plant and when to harvest would have been vital. Mother Earth, one imagines, would have been truly worshipped then. Perhaps it was around that time that inquisitiveness about the creation of the human child heralded conscious awe for the miracle of woman's ability to grow a baby from nothing. I can well believe that the inferior male would fall on his knees to worship such an event. Ancient female figurines still exist, indicating that this may have been the case in many places of the world. Perhaps these figurines represent God as Mother Earth?

As time passed, some inspired young scientist of the day must have declared that the sperm was the seed of life. The woman could then be relegated to merely the carrier of the man's offspring. *Homo sapiens*' society and beliefs may then have reflected the more masculine hunter-killer characteristics. Early rituals could easily have been further refined to include sophisticated forms of physical initiation ceremonies. These are acts that bind individuals into groups and increase tribal identity.

One can imagine that to be part of an exclusive worship club one had to reach puberty and undergo tests of bravery, often by way of bodily mutilation. Different tribes or groups adopted various patterns: teeth were filed; faces and arms were cut with razor-sharp bones or flints; hoops were used to stretch necks; lips were enlarged by inserting discs. The most common worldwide ritual required the genitals to be decorated or mutilated, normally in males by the removal of the foreskin. Amazingly many of these rituals still continue today, even in what are regarded as most sophisticated societies.

As the complexity of worship increased, what may have initially been an excuse for celebration became more and more part of a permanence to add to the growing cultural superstitions of successful human families.

The bonds formed through the rituals helped progress towards cooperation and the formation of independent tribes. Something, which may only have started out in a light-hearted manner, became like the modern-day National Lottery – an irrational addiction. Innocent pastimes changed into the domain of profit-and-power motivated organisers, who ensured their own wellbeing through the ritual of gift offerings and sacrifices.

Perhaps some tribes had a language that is still being echoed today. I can well imagine some of our ancestors claiming leadership by suggesting that there was a 'Fearsome Creative Force' that would only communicate to humanity through themselves.

This all-powerful god phenomenon may then have been further harnessed to destructive forces. Real fear of the often harsh, irrational physical world (floods, storms, volcanic action, tribal crises and so on) could be used by the unscrupulous to exert power over their fellow human beings. They could, for example, suggest that the supernatural controlling power was a *god*, or gods, of vengeance with whom they alone could negotiate.

I recollect as a child first coming across this god of revenge and punishment. I was about eight years old at the time and sitting in the front pew of Sunday School in Saint Hilda's Anglican Church in my home village of Griffithstown. My inquisitive eyes had led me up a broad, carved marble pillar seeking the source of a terrorizing voice high above me. There I saw a dreadful bat-like figure whose fiery eyes were trying to bore into my very skull. I sat there rigid with fright, aware of my clean clothes, my shining face, my hands folded in my lap according to my mother's instructions.

Apparently I was the source of evil, I had committed some sin that very morning, I would be found out, I would be eternally damned, I would be roasted in a fire! Perhaps I had not heard him properly? I tried to concentrate. I felt so very guilty. But what had I done? I could not remember even thinking anything bad, let alone doing it. Then there was all that strange talk about heaven being a reward for good behaviour. Surely to be good meant you were good simply because you loved to be good and enjoyed the pleasure of others all around you – not for some later reward?

I was shaken. For there was no place for the preacher's 'hell and damnation' within my understanding of a loving God.

So, it seems to me that our ancestors could well have made up descriptors of such a god – powerful, angry, wrathful, seeking vengeance, the mix spiced with convenient predictions such as that god will judge each one of us with a view to meting out punishment at some mystical time. This pattern certainly reflects much of mankind's desire to control others by fear. The history of human behavioural control and population subjugation is littered with such propaganda. On the other hand it could be that as some people developed true compassion and altruism, it gave them feelings of guilt, which led to ritual sacrifice being perceived as a cleansing mechanism.

The above contains much that can be observed in many belief systems today. There is clearly quite a strong case for assuming that the god phenomenon naturally developed from mankind's own history and imagination. Evolving human history is a fertile ground for those who believe that God is only a figment of human imagination. However, scenarios of past events will always contain a degree of conjecture. We cannot even be 100 per cent certain of the reason for ancient artefacts beside the dead; we can only make informed guesses. Yes, evolution is a strong contender but not an absolute proof of that initial spark which may have caused the mind of man to invent God.

We could investigate other branches of the evolutionary tree. There are countless historical possibilities that could account for mankind's belief in God. Even so, none are definite beyond all doubt. Therefore we cannot use mankind's historical development, or the theory of evolution, for the creation of the god phenomenon, as our *foundation* of absolute truth, for God may or may not be the guiding force behind such a complex system.

Could it be that, after all, the religious angle is the logical starting point for proof of the existence of God? Let's take a brief look at the second category contained within the traditions and beliefs of some world religions.

3.3 Scriptural Limits

Although I am a believer in the reality of God, I do not intend to allow this to influence my search for the truth. I trust that you will accept my apology in advance if, in the search for truth, I inadvertently insult your beliefs, for that is not my intention. That said, the scriptural God origin presupposes that ritual, superstition and human rules, under the guidance of God, were the prelude to mankind's belief in God. What then of the words of the religious masters, and the written records?

Do sacred texts themselves give us proof of the existence of God? That is, statements such as those found in Paul's New Testament letter to Timothy concerning the Jewish scriptures, 'All scripture is inspired by God', or could this simply be a circular argument of a text justifying itself? There is no doubt that world scriptures contain many pearls of human wisdom, from the simple day-to-day suggestions for living, to the more profound pointers of a transcendental reality. One way of releasing these 'pearls' is through prayer. For example, the following prayer came to me after I had meditated on many world scriptures, in particular the Holy Bible (Romans 8, Leviticus 19), the Guru Granth Sahib ji, the tract of the Quiet Way, the Book of the Dead, the Holy Qur'an, and Ravidas:

Almighty God, our heavenly Father, infinite in wisdom, love and power: May the children of this third millennium strive with all their strength and in deep humility to bring peace and harmony to all they meet. May the Holy Spirit help and reassure them through their weaknesses, so that with the gift of tears they become soldiers of prayer and peace, relieving all people in distress or danger.

Dear Lord, help each one of us to teach our children and grandchildren to love, to listen and to reason, to take responsibility for the poor and needy, to bear no grudge and to take no vengeance. May our future generations boast that they have not inflicted pain or injustice, but they have eliminated grieving, suffering, worry, sin, slavery and fear, so that all may find the eternal Kingdom of the Lord. May each one of us here today reflect on our human history and strive to leave the blessings of wisdom and prosperity with our children for all the generations to come.

O God, have compassion on those for whom we pray.

Even if we do not all agree that *prayer* is a meaningful practice, I suspect that the tenet of the above represents much that most of us would agree with.

Many adherents of different scriptural groups claim that scripture and/or the person who founded their religious belief system was in existence before time itself. Some faiths suggest that God referred to scripture before creating the universe.

The first religious group to make this latter claim can be found in the great Hindu scriptures, the Vedas, whose origin goes back into prehistory, long before the written word was invented. The Vedantic texts are believed, by many millions of people, to have been directly produced by God and given to selected people or seers. According to the Vedas, in the book of the Prasna Upanishad, the Vedic books themselves are used by God to recreate the universe at the beginning of each cycle of universal existence. This is best illustrated in Swami Nikhilananda's commentary on the First Question, when discussing the 'Universal Creator' (found in the translation of the Upanishads based on the commentary of the eighth-century philosopher Sri Sankaracharya),

Then through intense contemplation, which is called austerity, or tapas, the Creator awakens in His mind the subtle impressions of the Vedic knowledge acquired in His previous birth. With the help of that knowledge He sets about the task of creation.

The claim to pre-existence can also be seen in John's Gospel of the Christian New Testament: 'In the beginning was the Word, and the Word was with God, and the Word was God.' Here, most Christians believe that the Word is their founder Jesus.

The Sikh holy scriptures, the Sri Guru Granth Sahib ji, ensure that the 'Ultimate Reality' that they are speaking of is the one that existed first, for right on their first page they say of the 'Universal Creator': 'True in the prime, True in the beginning of ages.'

The scriptural texts could, of course, be true. By suggesting that the Word, the Ultimate Reality or the whole scripture came before the universe itself, the authors have taken the high ground; the position of being the initial source of knowledge and truth. Each religious group claims their own scriptures are authentic, inspired by or directly from God. Some groups go so far as to claim that *only their* scriptures are from God, implying that other revered texts are false. I believe that this latter claim is based more on the need for comfort and security, rather than a need to seek ultimate truth concerning the reality of God.

Many texts are taken in good faith by a large number of people as 'the word of God' given to mankind through a prophet, a seer, an enlightened one or a guru etc. Examples of one man influencing many can be found in Exodus from the Jewish Pentateuch. Here is just one,

So Moses came and called the elders of the people, and set before them all these words which the Lord had commanded him. And all the people answered together and said 'All that the Lord has spoken we will do'.

Moses must have been very convincing, for people apparently assumed that what he said was from the Lord, or God, and therefore absolutely true. We are told that Moses said this was the word of God, and that they believed him. Perhaps he had a direct revelation from God similar to that recorded in Paul's letters to the Galatians, where it is claimed that Paul's preaching was not taught to him by another human being but he 'received it through a revelation of the resurrected Jesus Christ.'

Many Jews, Christians and Muslims today believe that Moses actually conversed directly with God – God had actually instructed him. However, the only proof for those present when he came down from Mount Sinai (the Samaritans believed it was Mount Gerizim), was their knowledge of Moses' past record, a record that suggested amazing sacrifices, heartaches and miraculous happenings. For the people did not actually witness 'a conversation' between God and Moses.

It seems that extraordinary people or their followers have recorded countless billions of words (the equivalent of 50 Christian Bibles from the Buddha alone). These often claim exclusive instructions directly from the transcendental force, or God.

If one or all of these great works of God are truly authentic, i.e. the very hand of God, then our search is at an end, for we have found what led mankind to the concept of a god phenomenon, i.e. God alone did it.

If only this was uncontroversial and scripture showed no inconsistencies. Personally, however, the idea of God's 'hand', unblemished by human interjection, producing these writings has never completely satisfied me. Within the pearls of scriptural wisdom conundrums frequently occur which remind me more of the tactics employed by unscrupulous managers than the voice of God. Statements all too often smack of man's own selfish aims and ambitions. From the Book of Joshua, found in the biblical Old

Testament we learn that the Israelites set out to capture the walled city of Ai with 'some two or three thousand men'. Instead, they were routed. The leaders were puzzled, how could this possibly be? If God was with them, how could they have failed? As God was just, then the only explanation was that someone must have done something to offend the omnipotent Universal Creator. There could be no other explanation other than an admission that they had made the wrong decision in the first place. The leaders, at their wits' end, 'tore their clothes and flung themselves face downwards to the ground.'

Joshua their leader shouted out, 'Alas, Lord God, why did you bring this people across the Jordan just to hand us over to the Amorites to be destroyed?'

Biblical accounts submit that God answered,

'Israel has sinned: they have violated the covenant, which I laid upon them; they have taken things forbidden under the ban; they have stolen them; they have concealed them by putting them among their own possessions.'

A sceptic could surmise that this later 'revelation' was no more than a typical management technique of apportioning blame to one's own subordinates. The technique ensures that the subordinates feel guilt and remorse. Such an approach can actually enhance a manager's status, particularly if the manager has the authority to hire and fire – or in biblical terms 'forgive the transgressors'. Whatever the truth of the innermost thoughts of the leaders, records show that they succeeded in maintaining their control and led many more successful killing campaigns against their enemies.

This account of events in Jewish history being directly influenced by God cannot be ruled out; even so it is good to remember that blind faith can lead to a bloodbath. For 'killing for God' has been a recurring excuse behind so much human slaughter throughout history, and, sadly, still continues in many countries to this day.

And what of the scriptural contradictions, which continue to give rise to endless debate? In analysing and comparing different parts of the canonised Bible, one might expect to find consistency. But no, contradictions arise in both a micro and macro analysis. For example, there are considerable inconsistencies between the claimed characteristics of God found in the biblical books of Amos, Genesis, Psalms and Ruth.

That said, for me, God shines through many parts of these revered texts. We cannot ignore the fact that scriptures, such as the Christian Holy Bible, could in fact be true. However, I am far from being convinced that the original concept of a god came to mankind in the form of written text.

In the above I have given biblical examples, but controversy arises, to some extent, in all scriptures. How can the Holy Qur'an be thought of as unambiguous when some adherents of Islam interpret it as an excuse to kill and maim thousands of 'innocent' people, while the vast majority of those who live by the teachings of the same holy scriptures see in them a call to live in peace with others? Even if God does guide mankind, the mind of man, through which God speaks, inevitably contaminates, to some extent, the truth of God – just as a river in flood has its pure water discoloured with the mud from its banks.

For an atheist, scripture merely reflects mankind's growing imagination; for myself it is much more profound and points to God revealing truths to aid the developing consciousness of mankind. This is a viewpoint I intend to substantiate in a later book, but the first task must surely be to verify beyond all reasonable doubt that God is a reality.

World scriptures are definitely pointing to the reality of the transcendental. However, they cannot be the starting point or the *bedrock* when one reflects on the immeasurable imagination and complexity that the human mind can generate. It seems that we must broaden and continue our search.

3.4 Looking Inwards

Having taken a cursory look at the most popular arguments for and against the reality of God by considering our evolutionary origins and our religious heritage, we come to the last of the three categories, the 'Inner God', or what could be called 'Intuitive Awareness'. It is a personal approach to the origin of the god phenomenon.

Sherwin Nuland, in his book *The Wisdom of the Body*, limits the human spirit to a biological system containing wisdom and knowledge, and the only form of afterlife is an immortality which suggests that the world has changed, simply because you, or I, have been alive. We create a sort of 'non-existent afterglow'. According to Nuland there is no continuum of spirit, soul, self or consciousness, just continuing physical structures and processes which, once you are dead, you will never be aware of.

Modern psychologists suggest that the brain is not only responsible for logic, memory, emotion and the like, but also directly responsible for those phenomena experienced by humans, from visions to mass hysteria, from dreams to prophecy, in fact, all other forms of empathy and insight. For the most part, they have no truck with the existence of anything approaching psychic energy. They argue that it must be one of the most researched areas and yet there has never been any conclusive proof of other than mundane electro-biochemical action.

When we believe we have encountered God, are we then simply dealing with the mysteries of our own minds? Are the minds of humans so different from those of animals? Perhaps we have a level of consciousness that makes us desire to be part of an all-powerful human-like super-being. There are many things in our mechanistic world that could cause people to have a belief in God

without recall to any transcendental influence. Consider just four
cases:

- Most of us are born into a family, protected and cherished by
  our parents. What then would be more natural than to construct God as a perfect benefactor or parent?
- What about the fact that most people feel love towards their
  parents? This love may be independent of the actual love and
  kindness shown by the parents. I know numerous instances of
  tyrannical mothers bringing forth truly compassionate daugh-
  ters – my own loving mother being such a daughter. When children finally mature into true adulthood, love and care can well
  up from within them and they find they can accept their parents completely, warts and all, and strive to help and comfort
  them. This type of inner, caring emotion must be intrinsic and
  could lead us to the conclusion that we have some kind of creator who is love – a loving God.
- What of our need for friendship? Life can, at times, seem to be
  so lonely and insecure. I have seen many apparently happy, balanced people overcome by personal crises, and suddenly in
  need of a close, understanding and permanent friend. I believe
  that romantic notions which surpass the reproductive urge,
  and which have a basis in compassion, may be derived from
  this need for friendship. We all seek the perfect friend. As perfection seems to be a non-existent commodity among us
  humans, once again God, the ideal friend, is born in the minds
  of those in need.
- Then there is our need for heroes. For myself, in the 1940s and
  early 1950s, when stories of the second World War were still
  ringing in my young ears, I relished the exploits of ancient
  heroes like Hannibal and his Alpine elephants, Alexander and
  his road to India. When told of how a few hundred valiant
  Welsh soldiers kept at bay many thousands of fully armed, fear-

less, Zulu warriors my pride knew no limits. My heroes were all of flesh and blood, yet somehow they were beyond life itself, they were indestructible. What could be more heroic and unassailable than God?

Still others claim that God exists because certain patterns of their lives seem to them to be 'more than just coincidence', i.e. some form of transcendental phenomenon has been at work in their lives. This could be a true reflection, but how can we verify such claims?

We have a real problem here, for, as well as the problems cited above, there are countless reasons why someone else feels they have experienced God. To know what is truly in the heart and mind of another is not possible. Often we are not even sure of our own inner convictions. As the originator of the Sikh religion, Guru Nanak ji, pointed out, a Muslim, seemingly in devotional prayer, could in reality be thinking of his possessions, not of God.

I conclude that other people's experiences cannot be conclusive evidence for the reality of God, although their experiences may reinforce our own convictions.

As each of us looks inward, the experience we can perceive is unique to ourselves. Scientific investigations all seem to be about observing and changing the world 'out there', from music and art to the function of the brain and the depths of emotion – what about this inner world we each have, our private world, our individuality. It is our private world, which could well point us to the seemingly unfathomable truth of existence itself.

What am I? Looking inwards, into myself, I find that I am far from stable; I could be engrossed in loving thoughts when a dog unexpectedly barks so loudly that I physically jump, immediately dissolving my state of equilibrium, and I may even become aggressive.

Our reactions change with experiences of life. Some of these changes can be permanent. The changes can become a new way of thinking.

Going further into myself I encounter base instincts, for survival and the satisfactions of lust and greed. Then, other more philosophical thoughts arise.

I remember in my early grammar school years puzzling over Shakespeare's 'to be or not to be'. I felt that there was some hidden message in that simple statement, a sort of codified world, like the ones I encountered later on in my life when reading the Book of Revelation.

I may have moved a long way from my position of 50 or so years ago, but my attempt to capture, fully understand and convey the meaning contained in such a simple phrase as 'I am' is still with me. Perhaps this is the bedrock that other people have recognised down the ages. After all, when the Jews requested God's name, the answer they had was, 'I am that I am'. If only I can express this very state of 'I am', i.e. that which is my very *being*.

By *being* I don't just mean the realisation of my own body, mind, emotion and consciousness. I am trying to grasp something dimensionally beyond these things. *Being* is not being anything in particular. It seems to be linked to the self-reflecting conscious awareness that tells each one of us that we personally exist. 'I am' is such a simple concept, which nevertheless seems to defy explanation.

This *being* does not qualify my existence – it *is* my existence. How could *being* itself come into existence?

Investigations concerning how things are born or evolve and die or become extinct are today relatively straightforward. The question of the origin of *being* is much more difficult to grasp than that of, say, the origin of life, my psychology or my own biological origin. How can I understand the very *essence* of myself?

This realisation of self, which transcends the science of Einstein or the logic of Plato, has proved to be a most elusive concept for so many great minds. *Being* itself in one way is so simple, while in another it can stretch our understanding to breaking point.

Being is a deep selfhood that cannot be replaced by anything or anyone else. An identical twin is amazingly aware of his or her cognate, but he or she still has independent knowledge of his or her own existence. A programmed genetic 'clone' of myself, or the most complex super bio-computer of the future, with its ability to emulate my all would not, from my point of view, be 'me'. Even if it was perfected to such an extent that Jeanette, my wife and best friend of over 40 years, could not distinguish it from me, it would still appear to me as another person – a person which greatly added to the complexity of my life!

Can I tell if my understanding of this phenomenon of selfhood is the same for everyone? I cannot even know what thoughts simple physical concepts like 'apple' give to another person. (Is 'apple' something to eat; a sign of sexual promiscuity; a specimen for discovering gravity; a seed carrier; a plaything; the fruit which gave mankind the knowledge of evil; a health food; a thing to pack and store; an American City; death; a colour, shape or texture? Each concept has its own emotional baggage attached.)

I believe that the only absolute truth is not with anything bounded by the natural world, but is with *being* itself. Only the individual concerned can verify *being* for themselves. For, in the end, when we peel off all the philosophy we still know that our own existence is true even if nothing else is. And a search for understanding the reality of our own personal existence, or *being*, begs the question, 'What is the source of *being*' – is it the 'Great Light' which many call God?

Perhaps this personal idealised character is the basis of the god that so many believe in. Could this private god contain an absolute truth for *the start* of our endeavours to study the god phenomenon and 'mysteries' that give individuals direct revelations from God? Mysteries that include that part of the brain is specifically set aside for the 'religious experience'?

3.5 Seeking Bedrock

We have looked at origins of the human understanding of God, the god phenomenon, and divided the possibilities into three categories. We have been far from exhaustive, nevertheless, under the heading of the 'Evolving God', there were examples showing how the god phenomenon could have arisen as a natural, understandable concept occurring from within human imagination, ignorance, curiosity and the collective needs of the human psyche for certainties of life. Different experiences in different communities could have given rise to different starting points for the many societies who believe in the reality of God. Mankind's understanding of God could well be an evolving process, which may begin to suggest a reason for so many varied ideas about God.

Considering world religions and their scriptures, we have looked at the idea that God has implanted concepts concerning a transcendental reality in the minds of selected men and women. Scriptures, as we have noted, are filled with wonderful pearls of wisdom.

The first two categories certainly have more than a spark of truth both for and against the reality of God. Unfortunately absolute truth cannot necessarily be recorded history – secular or religious. For we cannot 'experience' evolution, nor will our reading of world scriptures give us an actual 'experience' of God and, as it was pointed out in the first chapter, experience is an essential element for any proof. Unfortunately, no matter how sincere other people's 'God experiences' seems to be, doubt concerning their authenticity can arise in our minds. Some of the evolutionary and scriptural scenarios are more plausible than others, but as an objective researcher (or some may say a sceptic), I cannot consider that they are necessarily *bedrock* – not the stable platform of timeless truth that I seek. However, if we succeed in establishing the fact that God exists, then it is most probable that both evolutionary and scriptural concepts will be a great help in establishing a fuller understanding of God.

It is within the third area alone, the 'Inner God' that there could be cause for optimism, for the fact that we are conscious of our own personal existence, or *being*, is not the same as the mechanistic world in which we find ourselves. All things we are aware of could be replaced and we could learn to adapt, all things that is, except our own very essence, our 'Greater Self', our very *being*. It is *being* that could be our link with a transcendental realty.

3.6 Opening the Door

As we consider the reality of our own personal existence, *being* itself, it can appear to be more and more difficult to conduct scientific investigations. Can I construct an experiment with *being* that will give me a true indication of the possibilities I am faced with that extend beyond the boundaries of conventional science?

At this juncture in our journey I am not attempting to relate *being* to the God that created the universe, conjured up the beauty of the countryside, allowed complex genomes and other patterns to evolve and is claimed to be the motivating force behind most world religions. I am aiming to verify that the transcendental exists, not to evaluate God or God's possible character.

If it is possible for us to conceive and carry out an experiment to prove the transcendental exists, it will be one experiment that we all have to enter into alone. For I believe that it is a form of transcendental experiment which is implied in the advice of people like the Buddha and other Indian mystics when they suggest that to find *truth* each one of us must evaluate the evidence for ourselves. Then there is the founder of Christianity, Jesus, who clearly tells us to find a quiet place and pray alone. It is this 'aloneness' that one must enter into first and discover the non-egocentric self, or as some would say the 'Greater Self', that which I am calling *being* itself. For this experiment to be meaningful we must accept that no one can substitute or help us. Only each one of us, individually, can show conclusively that *being* is the door to a deeper understanding of our human condition. Some people from Bangladesh have a saying for this bedrock of truth: 'You know when you have realised your "Greater Self" – for all doubts disappear permanently.' I have found it quite a task to remove all my doubts because of the inherent difficulty in focusing on *being*, and then moving on to begin to grasp its significance. It is from the experience of *being* that we will most fruitfully progress to realise the existence of the transcendental. To have such an experience will require us to have both an open heart and a cool head.

Naturally you may feel that you have already passed this point of understanding many times before. I would still recommend caution, for you may be like a colour-blind man who insists that he can see the rainbow as others do, but in reality he cannot see the full beauty of its myriad colours.

As previously suggested, realising the transcendental, like scientific facts, must be experienced. Unlike many discoveries in science that I accept are true, I have found that I have had to experience the transcendental for myself to be convinced of its reality. Thus as both evolution and world religions are doubtful starting points for our journey, any definitive proof of the reality of God must, of necessity, be by our own personal experience. This suggests that to find out if God exists or not, we may have to further develop our own experiential ability, especially our ideas concerning assessing such experiences. It is most important not to be deceived, and to be certain that it is a transcendental experience that we are apprehending. We need a self-validating experience, one that carries its own guarantee of infallibility. All in all, a very tall order.

If we choose to live with and love a life-long partner, the mind is given plenty of reinforcing evidence that you are together from experiences from intense disagreements to feeling unbounded love for your partner who is sleeping by your side. However, when we look inwards there is unlikely to be any external collaboration. We may be able to describe an external object like an oak tree in sufficient detail for us all to agree and even get a third party to draw it. But describing the inner understanding of one's own consciousness is much more difficult. For this experiment we will need to consider tuning our own mind. For some this sensitivity to the transcendental may be a natural gift, but for many of us external props are a great help. It is only our own mind and con-sciousness that we can use to detect transcendental reality.

3.7 Defining an Elementary Experiment

An experiment is a tentative procedure in order to test or establish an hypothesis. A 'God-experiment' requires us in some way to focus our minds on our own consciousness and follow our consciousness to the point where enlightenment first dawns. To where 'I am' becomes a profound understanding.

Most of us can remember our school days when an experiment consisted of:

• An aim or objective,
• Something to work on (a specimen),
• Something to work with and measure outcome (the apparatus),
• A clearly defined method which includes such things as environmental requirements,
• Conclusions.

What I need is an elementary procedure, which if conscientiously carried out will allow an experience of a transcendental reality devoid of any religious or other bias; an experience of 'the breath of God', or 'the grace of God', or 'the presence of the holy spirit', or a merging with 'the greater consciousness'.

A formal experiment is a way of recreating conditions to give results. I believe that such results occur naturally, in experiences most of us have had when we were young. I remember as a youth on the hillside above my home town becoming filled with overwhelming empathy then attempting to express my deep knowledge of beauty, awe, wonder and oneness by bursting into a rather poor rendering of 'to wake up in the morning to the mocking bird's song'. What was it that so filled me with awe? How can I recreate, at will, such a condition of my mind and consciousness? This basic 'calling out' or setting up of an experimental environment where all one's senses are alert yet open and ready to be dissolved into an understanding experience of *being* is perhaps the simplest yet the most profound of life's experiences. There are many other more complex experiences that point directly to the reality of God, but we will leave these until the next chapter.

So, having discussed our aim, and decided that the 'something to work on' is *being* itself, what apparatus will we use?

3.8 The Apparatus

There is no need to acquire an engineering degree to drive a car; similarly there is no need to know how the brain may receive transcendental data to experience God. The question we should be asking ourselves does not concern the physical working of the brain but, 'can we carry out a "door-opening" experiment which will show us a platform of truth, or bedrock, from which we can develop and explore more fully the reality of God?' This is a good point to briefly review a few salient points concerning our 'experimental apparatus' which, I hope you'll agree, is the mind itself.

There seems little doubt today that all our thinking, memory, emotion, reasoning and perception is, whether conscious or unconscious, located in the brain. Even the emotions of love, hate, fear, jealously, anger and so on, are no longer found in the rhythm of our heartbeat. It is all in that grey matter in our skulls. So it would seem obvious that we can only know the reality of God through conscious thought. Just as all scientific and other 'facts' can only be known when we become conscious of them so our knowledge of God can only be known when we become conscious of God.

Functionally the brain consists of a biologically active network of 100,000,000,000, (one hundred billion) neurons, communicating with each other. Science, so far, has discovered that this communication contains both electrical and chemical signals. Axons and dendrites interface at the synaptic junctions causing a neuron to fire when it receives a signal of about 40mV, (three or four hundred times smaller than the voltage of a car battery). The brain's central nervous system has attributes that can be measured using modern instrumentation. It is just about possible to detect individual neurons firing in the brain.

To me it is truly amazing that we can detect such small amounts of radiation, emitted by just one neuron, especially when one considers that Marconi only sent and received the first 'wireless' Morse coded signal as recently as 1901. At the time there was little understanding of this unseen radio energy (electromagnetic radiation, or e-m radiation), even though all things have radiated e-m energy since the beginning of time – from galaxies to the simplest substances, including all the life forms of the natural world.

By comparing the brain with the radio perhaps we can have a better understanding of the limitations of conventional brain measurements. No one would suggest that because you can get an output from a radio by forcing an electric signal somewhere in its amplifying circuits, this proves the radio is intrinsically incapable of receiving external information. Why then, do some people tell us that forcing signals into the brain and measuring the effects (or simply measuring brain activity), will tell us the complete story of the mechanistic brain, let alone the complexity of the mind and consciousness? There are such things as meditative prayer and other cognate activities, which, at times, show results that seem to be inexplicable using known physical principles. Perhaps one day we may discover 'super fine' tuning circuits of the receiver of the mind by which we receive human empathetic understanding or, more to the point in this case, transcendental information. But, first we would have to discover what form of energy, or otherwise, any external information carrier, detectable by the brain, could possibly be.

We simply do not know if there is any form of receiver in the mind – that is at present beyond our understanding. It is, perhaps, worth reminding ourselves that many eminent scientists, philosophers and businessmen laughed at Marconi and his concept of communication without wires, light or sound – and they were *all* wrong!

What types of energy or states of matter are still around waiting to be discovered? Perhaps the e-m radiation that Marconi used is the clearest indication that there are likely to be other phenomena that we have still to discover, understand and utilise. Not detecting an e-m energy source associated with psychic energy does not prove or disprove anything. The jury is still out, and if we insist on verification using only the kind of energy with which science is at present familiar, the jury may never come back in.

3.9 The Method

The method is aimed at invoking a required reaction when we 'desire' it, not in a random fashion, as is the case for most report-ed transcendental experiences. This can be achieved by elemen-tary meditation, but to increase the chances of success I suggest the use of a catalyst. The catalyst itself will often be quite breath-taking and care must be taken not to become overwhelmed by it. For example, music, such as that of Debussy, which captures the special rarefied ambience of a gull in flight, may appear to be a wonderful catalyst. For music inhabits some special place in our psyche that seems to allow us to drift in the free-fall of the mys-tical world of the composer and player. However, such a catalyst is already 'contaminated' for it fills the mind with someone else's ideal. It can so easily point us 'outwards', and in so doing lock us into worldly awesomeness. To comprehend that which is beyond our senses, the transcendental, we must be travelling 'inwards'. So, although at first sight music appears to unlock the secrets of the soul, in fact it limits experience to the beauty found within, or very accessible by, the conscious realm.

So I will try and explain an early 'experiment' which acted as a catalyst and 'opened the door' for me. It occurred in the winter of 1978, at the mountain hamlet of Cefn-y-Crib in Gwent where my wife, Jeanette, and I had opted for the 'good life'.

We had several years previously taken our two children from the material luxury of the prospering Medway towns of Kent and, as our son, Jonathan, later joked, 'dumped them on the barren, alien environment of the upper Welsh hills.' As a family we had survived in two small caravans while reuniting two sad stone cottages, iso-lated on a few acres of land. Land abandoned by time on the slopes of a water-formed valley. Abandoned too, it seems, by man – a hidden valley.

All was going well; we now inhabited beautiful restored cottages and lived the 'good life', surrounded by geese, chickens, pigs, ducks, rabbits and an abundance of organically produced food – we even used our old Welsh cob, Sunset, to plough! Things seemed to have reached a peaceful equilibrium.

It was a very late evening in February. I was slumped in front of the glowing log fire. My senses were becoming dulled, succumbing to the warm caresses that were lulling my weary body into peaceful sleep. But the tumbling thoughts, which were switching through my mind, would not rest. Ideas moving, changing, alive with the practical work of the smallholding. Soon all subsided into a different world. What was the meaning of it all? Thoughts of worldly aims dissolved as I uninhibitedly allowed my naked mind to search for hidden truths in the comforting sea of my own consciousness. Within my simple meditations came persistent pulses which urged me to be completely alone, to be outside, away from the comfort of my home and family.

I struggled to put on my father's long, thickly-lined railway coat as I greeted the night air. No longer enclosed by the cottages I walked around in the still blackness of the night. The blackness soon faded to reveal the frozen world. Into my contemplative thoughts the words of one of Jeanette's favourite Christmas carols, 'earth as hard as iron,' hummed its way through my mind. I reflected how, earlier that day, I had used a five-foot metal fencing bar and still had been unable to prise up parsnips from their slumber in the concrete earth.

As the hills, the trees, then the hoarfrost grass revealed their crystalline forms my mind once more subsided into its own consciousness. Somehow I was also in deep, clear empathy with the majesty of the heavens. The moon, the clouds, even the air it seemed, had left the night to the stars – the Seven Sisters, the Plough, the North Star...

My body was still cosy and sleepy from the fire. My mind, filled with kaleidoscopic wonder was sharp and clear, as it rested in tranquillity, a null-point of perfect peace.

I sat, then lay, on the frozen earth, alone. Above me I could see countless points of light cascading across the heavens. Awesome! I could feel the Earth turning so very slowly, so very silently, so very smoothly. I was alone – all alone.

I could not move – the planet held me with its immense strength. I was pinned to the ground. Completely open-hearted, my mind in perfect harmony floated free among the stars and galaxies. Then it happened...

I became profoundly aware that I *was* the stars, the hills, the grass. I went beyond deep empathy – I was the *all*, for *all* was one. I fused with the all, and was blessed with understanding.

Did I experience the Vedic harmony which, 'is established between the personal and the universal nature of this vision'? Perhaps the poet Wordsworth, recorded in his Ode, 'Imitations of Immortality,' experienced the same profundity as I did on that clear February night, when he wrote:

Of the eternal Silence: truths that wake,
To perish never
Our souls have sight of the immortal sea
Which brought us hither...'

Was I part of the 'Great Silence'? That inner silence described in Paul's letter to the Philippians as, 'the peace of God which is beyond all understanding.'

It seems that one must:

Take thyself into your own heart.
Love not the perfected things of yourself,
Love your very existence.

I could go on and try and explain more of this experience, but perhaps it has been described sufficiently for you to think of it as an example of an elementary, yet profound experiment. It has been recorded firstly to help to clarify what an elementary transcendental experience is. And secondly as a possible aid, to encourage you to enact an experiment for yourself.

You may find, like me, that a natural setting is the source for your own catalytic experience, where you can *feel secure, clear-headed, open-hearted and at the same time humble.* Experiencing intensity such as I am struggling to express is truly mystical; it involves losing yourself and becoming infused with the vitality that is all around you. It is like the blind seeing, the deaf hearing or the clinically depressed suddenly appreciating the surging life of youthful spring.

Naturally your first experience may be even more dramatic than that elementary, religiously unbiased one of mine, described above. There are countless examples of life-changing experiences for many people who sincerely seek the truth, or have reached a point in their lives when they call out to God.

For some it is a specific cry to God. Such as the cry of despair from Bill W's lips when he felt utterly finished and helpless under his addiction for alcohol, the 'demon drink':

All at once I found myself crying out, 'If there is a God, let Him show himself! I am ready to do anything, anything!' Suddenly the room lit up with a great white light. I was caught up on an ecstasy, which there are no words to describe. It seemed to me in my mind's eye, that I was on a moun-tain and that a wind not of air but of spirit was blowing. And then it burst upon me that I was a free man...

Bill W had let go. He was completely changed by his experience and in 1935 became the founder of that worldwide organisation, Alcoholics Anonymous (AA). Today it has over a million members. But Bill's experience is, in some respects, a random transcendental experience of the kind that we will discuss in the next chapter.

3.10 Conclusion

I have found that the only bedrock of absolute truth lies *within* each one of us and is not part of the external world in which we live. It is beyond conventional science, world history and religion. The bedrock is experiencing that which created your essence, or *being*. It is experiencing 'the breath of God'.

If you succeed, or have succeeded in the past, in passing the barrier into experiencing *being* you will know, and the exhilaration will far exceed balancing on your first bicycle or even experiencing that breathtaking moment of perfect intimacy between yourself and the person you love.

All so very different from being a critical observer or bystander.

You experience a cataclysmic change – you have a new worldview. Amazingly these moments of deep insight, moments of deep truth, are often forgotten among the distracting pressures of our everyday lives. I try not to forget mine.

By exposing ourselves wholeheartedly to transcendental moments the full dawn of a realisation of *being* will break and the 'Greater Self' will begin to be exposed. The elementary experiment in essence is a silent inner journey of understanding. The realisation of the 'Greater Self' is where all doubts disappear and the 'experimental' results are as clear to you as, for example, the change of colour observed when lead becomes lead oxide (grey to red). You *know* when you have realised this 'Greater Self' for it becomes a repeatable result. Moreover, it will be a *humbling* experience, which fills you with a *spiritual* strength, and become an unshakeable truth for you for the rest of your life.

This 'totality of awareness' could occur at any time and at any place from snow-capped mountain peaks to seeing a traffic-light change. It is the consistency and repeatability of the knowledge of the awesomeness of your own existence that results from this personal experiment, and which gives an inner awareness. Knowing that your own existence or being is a fact at the level I am trying to express will constitute irrefutable bedrock for you, and you will know that a transcendental reality exists. The repeatability is not the awesomeness of the natural catalyst (such as my example or, say, being present at the birth of your first child). The breathtaking realisation of *being* punches right through one's normal level of consciousness. It is this repeatability that ultimately shows you, the experimenter, that experiencing *being* and the 'Greater Self' is not simply a subjective, one-off experiment. It is in fact the basis for a platform of absolute truth. A platform from which one can begin to explore the meaning of a transcendental reality, and begin to arrive at some understanding of that which created 'self' and *being*, that which many call God.

The elementary transcendental experience as described above, can be planned and tried by anyone who in all *humility and with deep sincerity* seeks truth with patience and perseverance. The more advanced transcendental experiences, for most of us, come later.

This truly amazing reality is the beginning of a journey within the 'transcendental plane'. For some it is what they have always known, for others it is like being born again. It is a journey of stunning kaleidoscopic colour beyond the mirage of the rainbow and can lead us into a journey of infinite understanding where truth upon truth can pile up before our inner eye. It is the tuned mind passing through an opened door from the world of everyday science into the world of the science of God. It is the food of the prophets, seers, gurus and the Son of God.

In the next chapter we will investigate and seek to categorise experiences which border on the transcendental.

Chapter 4

Experiencing God

This chapter uses several 'case studies' to illustrate possible categories at the boundaries of the transcendental experience.

4.1 Introduction

All my life I have sought the truth concerning the reality of God. Sometimes there are flashes of blinding insight, at other times, no matter how much I desire it, nothing remotely transcendental happens.

This could be because seeking the reality of God is so very different from performing most scientific observations of, say, a prepared specimen slide. In this case the object of our search has to, in some respects, 'decide to visit' us! God cannot be contained and brought out for inspection whenever we feel like it.

Although I believe that God is always present, in one way seeking God is like trying to observe a very shy animal, which only occasionally comes to the watering hole for a drink. In this respect our more advanced experiments within the 'science of God' are by definition similar to naturalists or zoologists looking for a rare animal to see if it truly exists and what it is like.

As we venture into the transcendental we have to be extremely careful when recollecting our experiences of the wider perception of our minds and be on guard against any interpretation that might contain hidden agendas. I am thinking here about the people who often hijack these wider experiences by suggesting that they are unique to their own brand of belief, which may be religious, agnostic, atheistic, humanistic or even philosophical.

In the main, transcendental experiences are one-off events. Memorable snapshots, similar to the one and only time I saw a kingfisher from my boathouse home by the river Taff in Cardiff – they cannot be repeated at will.

Throughout history, sudden and dramatic religious conversions have occurred. Mystical experience is more common than is generally admitted, even though the interpretation of such experiences varies from individual to individual.

What are we to make of Hugh Montefiore's, the then Anglican Bishop of Birmingham, reported 'visionary experience' – that of seeing and hearing Jesus when he was at Rugby school? His was only a fleeting experience; nevertheless it shaped the rest of his life. Then there are those such as that of a London bishop, whom I had the privilege of meeting on one of the Annual Interfaith Peace walks in the British capital. When he was twelve years old, at a Billy Graham revival, he 'simply' asked for Jesus to come into his life, a request that he assured me was granted and has been permanent. What of the great historical figures who had such astounding experiences that not only fundamentally changed their own lives but went on to affect the lives of millions of other people. Such as that 'ordinary' Indian who became the great nineteenth-century guru known as Ramakrishna after he 'saw' a small flock of cranes flying overhead. Or the founder of the Sikh religion, Guru Nanak ji, who, when he was only a boy, completely disappeared for three days and later claimed to have been with God. Or the son (Gautama) of a fabulously rich landowner, who after his conversion became a mere beggar, later to be known by countless millions as the Buddha.

I could recount many first-hand discussions with people who seem to have had very real experiences ranging from poltergeists to what science terms mass hysteria. They could be pointers to a transcendental reality, but I will always have reservations about their authenticity, as they are, for me, other people's experiences.

I am naturally very aware that the human mind can easily be tricked. Take for example the Cambridge astronomer James Challis who distrusted altogether the hypothesis of Leverrier and Adams concerning the existence of a new planet. He actually sighted the hypothetical planet four times during the summer of 1846 and once even noticed that it appeared to have a disc around it. Even so it did not register with him as it made no impression on his closed mind. Challis reported that there was no such 'new planet'. It was only much later, when others had seen and recorded the existence of Neptune that, on re-analysing his data, he realised that he had actually seen the new planet, but it had left no impression on him. His mind had refused to accept the truth.

To pinpoint a little more accurately just what a transcendental experience is, I would now like to consider everyday experiences, those which are hard to explain and those which cannot be explained without recourse to some form of transcendental reality. I call these three areas: *Normal, Boundary and Transcendental* experiences. To help to clarify these three types of experience I will use my own experiences simply as a set of illustrative case studies. (Bear in mind that eventually the fact has to be faced that any worthwhile study of the 'Science of God' demands that you, yourself, record and think through your own experiences.)

The first type of experiences, *Normal*, include the innovative and inspired modes of the mind. They represent the normal functions of the human mind, nevertheless some suggest they are from a transcendental source, a viewpoint that I have some sympathy with.

The second category of experience form a Boundary between *Normal* and *Transcendental*, where there is some doubt about their origination. They may or may not have transcendental connections.

The third are experiences that leave no room for doubt, they involve more than the simple bio-electromagnetic functions of the brain/mind alone. They are definitely of a *Transcendental* nature.

To eliminate the many modes of mental activity which could produce illusions within the mind itself I have confined the case studies to what I consider to be a fully alert mind. Topics such as nightmares, and so-called demonic, or evil forces, have not been included, neither has spiritual healing. These topics demand a book of their own; also I have come to believe that they would add little to our fundamental quest – that of verifying the actual existence of God.

Throughout the following experience-rich journey (the next eight sections), it must be emphasized that they are all true, but are only intended to help to clarify the definition of my three chosen categories of experience *(Normal, Boundary, Transcendental)*.

4.2 The Subconscious

A typical *Normal* subconscious experience is when the subconscious mind is working away in the background of our thoughts.

In my youth I discovered a marvellous aid to passing exams. I initially read through the exam paper and let the so-called subconscious beaver away at a difficult question while my mind concentrated on another easier question. When I returned to the question that I had previously found difficult, (my active mind having been completely occupied with answering the easier questions), I often found that my subconscious had conveniently lined up the solution for me.

I don't think I am unique in this respect, I suspect that it is a natural technique available to all who wish to exploit it.

4.3 Advanced Innovation

A *Normal* advanced innovation experience is when an idea suddenly floods into the mind that is not consistent with a progressive, step by step, series of logical thoughts, often with quite a profound outcome. It could simply be fully contained within the computer-like functions of our physical brain, or it could be the mind linking with the infinite, something beyond the conscious or the subconscious although I believe that the former is the most likely explanation for these experiences.

Perhaps the great mathematician Poincaré, describing his experience of sudden insight indicates what I am driving at:

...The changes of travel made me forget my mathematical work. Having reached Coutances, we entered an omnibus to go some place or other. At the moment I put my foot on the step the idea came to me, without anything in my former thoughts seeming to have paved the way for it, that the transformations I had used to define the Fuchsian functions were identical with those of non-Euclidean geometry.

This is the advanced innovation that comes unexpectedly and leaps over normal scientific progression. It does not follow on from any logical sequence but jumps straight to the answer. It is as if solutions arrive spontaneously in the cortex and the conscious mind manages to grab hold of them before they fade away. It may take considerable time afterwards to prove that the original instantaneous, inspired, intuitive solution was an eminently suitable way to solve a problem.

As I can only be sure of my own experience I will illustrate this category with a personal example, which occurred in my early professional work and happened to me when I was a young engineering student in the early 1960s. I had managed to obtain a job near the Elstree Film Studios at Borehamwood, just north of London. The concept of an aircraft in-flight recorder, the 'black box', had not been with us long, and was only available in a few, mainly military, aircraft. The problem that I was asked to look at was interfacing the aircraft transducers with the black box itself. It had been proved feasible by using transformers, which intrinsically required a relatively large amount of iron in their -up.

Now, minimum weight and size are of the essence in aircraft design and what was called for was a light, small solution. I had been set a typical 'unsolvable' problem for a newcomer – something to keep me quiet and occupied for a few weeks, until I could be slotted into a more permanent project. Numerous American firms had been unable to solve this problem – even my own Managing Director, Ron Bristow, a first-rate professional engineer had failed.

After a fruitless week I was near to giving up, especially as I was aware that much greater minds than mine had not solved the problem. Then, without any progressive thoughts or analysis, a very simple solution 'presented' itself in my mind.

The solution was to build in a definite error at the outset by assuming that sections of the electrical output from aircraft control systems were linear, when everyone concerned knew that they were not, (in reality they were the elegant curves of a sinusoidal waveform). This successful approach to practical design was, for me, unique and against all the fundamental principles I had been taught. Months later the solution proved to be completely successful using light compact electronic components to replace the heavy and cumbersome transformers. Naturally things have moved in leaps and bounds since that time, but the last time I visited the British Museum my sub-assembly system was still being exhibited. And the principle, as far as I am aware, is still used today throughout the world of aviation.

These types of experiences are not confined to scientific innovation and invention. They are, I believe, related to the inspiration of Michelangelo, the music of Elgar, the literature of Shakespeare, the poetry of Wordsworth and perhaps even receiving the grace of the 'Holy Spirit'. By that I mean that advanced innovation may not be of our 'own' making but more a gift given to us; even so we will take a conservative approach and consider it a normal internal function of the brain.

4.4 Inspiration

Inspiration is where ideas flow into the mind. It can take many forms; in this case I will give an example of the inspiration that arises out of observing a natural phenomenon. This is still most likely to be a *Normal* experience.

This particular experience occurred at our boathouse home in Llandaff. It was the summer of 1992. From the lounge I looked down at the almost motionless river which, due to the summer growth of trees, appeared to have become a large pond, a pool of tranquillity. The movement of its surface was barely perceptible as the waters silently slipped past. The pool, a dark tinted mirror, reflected the stone walls and lush growth of the surrounding banks.

Quite unexpectedly a perfect white swan glided in a straight line across the glassy stillness. The water, in recognition of the swan's passage, formed itself into its inevitable radiating fan. Harmonious waves wrote a complete history of the swan's passing as they stretched out to the grassy riverbanks.

I smiled as I imagined the ripples getting smaller and smaller as time moved on, but never *quite* fading away, for they were determined by the exponential functions of mathematics and would, in theory, last forever. Theoretically, people would be able to see the results of these reverberating ripples on the surface for evermore, and possibly be able to reconstruct their initial conditions, by simply analysing the minute ripples remaining on the glassy surface.

Then, the swan was gone. Like time it had passed on its way. The water appeared once more to be an immeasurable stillness. The pool was ready to be painted upon again.

But my mind would not rest. It floated on through thoughts of the exponential nature of the pond ripples. Would the most sensitive instruments still be able to recreate, from the dying reverberations of the pond's surface, those *first* ripples of that majestic swan? How long would I need to analyse the surface, if all of the most sensitive equipment that I could possibly conceive were at my disposal instantly: the transducers, the computers, and the army of scientists...? The morning breeze gently rippled the water.

Could I ever recreate the swan's wake? Would I be forever producing an infinite series of possibilities? Even if I did succeed in recreating the complete movement of the water when the swan passed, and recognised that it was the significant pattern that I sought, could I ever prove the existence, and beauty, of that which created the pattern – the swan? For the swan is not of the dimension of water...

My mind floated on. I realised that I might theorise on the origin of the universe or my own biological journey through time. I might observe and record the natural attributes of such things as water (movement, colour, acidity etc). But I would never, ever, find in such things 'the swan', that 'Creative Force' which I am calling God.

The swan unexpectedly appeared once more, moving with infinite grace. It seemed to have sublime knowledge of many things that the water could not recall. And my mind held the thought: 'Look inward to your heart, meditate on that which is there, find the window over your river, don't stare at the curtain, open it, believe and expect the unexpected – you will be rewarded.'

The thoughts that came to me with this inspirational experience told me that it was not the water that I should analyse; rather it was the swan itself. Thus to find God I must become more in tune with God. The experience showed me that there are many beautiful things to share in this life and that the mysteries we encounter go beyond the physical world. I felt that I had so clearly been

shown why no one could verify the reality of God using any arte-
fact, someone else's personal experience, or for that matter conventional science.

4.5 Simple Visions

The following example is for me a *Boundary* experience. By *Boundary* I am inferring that while some of us would view such an experience as a *Normal* action of a biochemical brain, others would consider it to be of a *Transcendental* (beyond the mind alone) nature.

When I was thirteen years old I felt that I had been personally given a glimpse of God. It must have been in the summer of 1952.

My eighteen-year-old sister, Joan, had brought her latest boyfriend home to be viewed by the family. He was a quiet, thoughtful student from Bristol University and he had come to stay at our little terraced house on the slopes of the South Wales hillside town of Griffithstown.

For some long-forgotten reason, I found myself walking with him across the country road towards the neighbouring village of New Inn. We were near the river Afon Llwyd, which myth had told us once had fish in it. Now it was a black slimy open sewer, which announced its presence by its putrid smell. I courageously broke the silence with, 'Do you believe in God?' – courageous because in those days when details of sex were readily available, the description of God was a very closely guarded, adult secret.

It seemed to work; first he started talking about a Utopia where we all shared and people had whatever they wanted. Then, to my surprise, he asked *me* what God was like.

'Don't know,' I replied for I had hoped that a man from the University would render to me a great outpouring about God, but no, he simply insisted that as I seemed to believe in God then I *must* have a picture of Him.

What was my picture? I fell silent, disappointed.

My mind revived a little – this could be the moment – if I could conjure up a picture for him, to show my understanding, he would obviously use it to illustrate God. This could be some sort of initiation test that I had to pass.

I had to think hard. I had to think fast.

This was it; this was the vital time!

The stink of the river filled my nostrils and seemed to fill my very being.

I hesitated again, for God had no form to me. Even so, he insisted, what was my picture of God? I concentrated really hard, (perhaps my first meditative prayer?) and I seemed to relax into a void.

A picture came – no, not a picture – more a complete three-dimensional world.

I was oblivious to all else. It was clear, it was beautiful, and it was complete. There was no colour in front of me, only purity in the form of fluffy cumulus clouds – a warm, tapering corridor of cloud.

Sitting at the far end was a man. Old in wisdom, young in stature. He had long flowing hair and beard; both as white as new-blown snow. His eyes were of love and warmth, his ageing face was moulded by the elements of everything – it glowed, not with anything tangible, but with the compassion of knowing, of caring, of hoping that we would all understand – understand that life was but a game and he was the master. The teacher who wanted – so much – for everyone to win, to enjoy, to be filled with a deep knowledge of truth. His whole form was crystal clear and still, somehow he was part of the pure white clouds.

Light did not come from behind or above him or from him, yet all was bright. He was not mythical light but human! Sitting on a throne of cloud.

This was God! ...

I blurted out: 'He's a man, with a white beard on a big throne.'

My heart pounded for his answer. 'That's a lot of rubbish,' was all I heard.

We walked on in silence, the silence that allows one to cope with inner inexpressible thoughts.

My 'picture' now seems more like one of the Byzantine ceiling frescoes that I have seen in the great churches of Venice, with God as a cross between Michelangelo's *Moses* and William Blake's *The Ancient of Days*. God's knowing face seemed to capture the *Mona Lisa* of Leonardo Da Vinci while showing the exuberance, the joy of Jean-Baptiste Carpeaux's *The Dance*. And yet my home boasted only three or four books and such art was not among them. My picture of God at the time far surpassed anything that I had any remote memories of. Although it now sounds rather typical of many 'childish' images I am still moved by its memory.

Could this very human picture of a separate being – God – be used as a basis for analysis? Was I lucky to be given such a benevolent glimpse of God? Or was it all simply an overactive imagination? Again there are so many possibilities. For me, as I had the experience, it represents a *Boundary* between that which is the normal functioning of a mechanical mind and that which could turn out to be *Transcendental*.

4.6 Flowing Empathy

I would now like to share with you a different kind of experience, which is hard to categorise as *Normal* or *Transcendental*. I will therefore refer to this also as a *Boundary* experience.

It was in early summer 1992. Jeanette and I were touring the vineyards of southern France. We were in Provence, not far from the sheer rock faces of the Verdon Gorges. We had decided to visit Moustiers Sainte-Marie for the day.

The small hamlet of Moustiers Sainte-Marie has had a chequered past and was described by one popular guidebook as, 'the Hell hole of tourism.'

We came expecting nothing. It was the usually quiet June that one experiences before the onslaught of the official French tourist season.

The town was like a limpet on the side of a thousand feet of awesome rock. Perched even higher, hundreds of feet above the town, was the church of Notre Dame de Beauvoir, accessible by a precarious meandering footpath.

The church and town had seen it all, from being the prayerful tool of the early monks to 'noblemen' who, after creating daily hell for the surrounding peasants, prayed there – to ensure their place in heaven. More recently it has been the haunt of the pilgrims, the travellers and the seekers. Today it is mostly the preserve of the probing bustling ones clutching their 'sacred' digital and video cameras, pausing long enough to secure little holiday mementoes.

I climbed, then stopped for a moment just outside the little church with its wooden barrier and a faded notice requesting silence. I was intensely aware of the tremendous toil, sweat, pain and perseverance that must have taken place to succeed in building a church on that most inaccessible rocky ledge. As I pondered, the engineering problems that the builders must have faced melted into insignificance compared with the human motivation that would have been necessary before such an impossible building site could have been developed. In the mists of my thoughts I could begin to imagine the driving force, the vision, the keen eyes, the bright faces, the searching souls.

Walking into the church, where no light seemed to penetrate, I slowly became aware that towering over me to my left was a massive statue of Christ on the cross. There was water running out of crumbling plaster, plaster that covered walls of solid rock. The church was more like a cave, arching some 50 or 60 feet above my head and disappearing in a tunnel of gloom. Where I anticipated an altar at the far end, I saw only the dim outline of what appeared to be a massive, gilt monstrosity, gleaming menacingly in the darkness, its grotesque form practically filling the whole of the end of the tunnel. At the centre was a large dark blue oblong, which for some reason reminded me of the blackness of Hell itself. I forced myself to walk towards it, my primitive senses of survival on full alert.

I groped for a seat, sat down and closed my eyes – unsure of what I was confronting in that all-pervading gloom. Soon, to my surprise, I became aware that tumbling out all around me was warm love and care. Out of the building itself, out of the centuries, something benevolent was showering onto me, filling me with inner tranquillity and overwhelming peace. I became aware of a spiritual clarity, which emanated from the very structure of that 'insignificant' shrine high on the hill.

My thoughts and dreams became almost visionary as they passed in front of my seemingly all-knowing mind. Things long past and forgotten became clear and present. I remembered many of the Baroque gilded masterpieces that are to be found in churches all over Europe, each full of the craftsman's loving touch – simply intended to express, in a physical craft, a heavenly atmosphere that would help to uplift the souls of all who passed by.

Swimming thoughts continued to flow through my receptive mind as I sat motionless.

In memory of my gambling father, I had recently visited the world's most famous casino at Monte Carlo. A virtual palace built for profit, built for gambling, built to impress. Yes, the skills were majestic, the architect talented beyond anything that I could ever produce. Why was it so? I felt at that time that I would never really know the truth behind any human achievement. When I had stopped in that magnificent casino my consciousness sensed an emotional presence that was almost tangible. It was an emotional presence that filled me with tears and gave me a yearning to help the misguided and addicted gamblers in the casino. To help them understand that their lives should not be frittered away until the dying ends of youth left them helpless in the twisted body and defective mind of old age.

What did these thoughts mean? I am not sure. However, I do know that at that moment in the church of Notre Dame de Beauvoir there was a fundamental difference. I could feel love, blessedness, caring and compassion, but now it was all *coming* to me. Welcoming my soul with its understanding and knowledge. If only all people could feel as I did then, so deeply warmed and blessed.

As my mind cleared and I started to open my eyes, a complete, unexpected, personal prayer came to me. It simply said: 'Dear God. Help me to persevere on the path of your purpose.' Then my eyes snapped fully open to find the church all lit up. The gilt in front of me shone radiantly, the blue rectangle was clear – containing a beautiful form of the Madonna and child with twinkling stars all around them – yet no one had turned on the light.

Whereas one can easily explain the 'switching on' of the light in terms of my eyes adapting to the change in light intensity, it is immeasurably more difficult to comprehend the significance of the unexpected compassion flowing to and from oneself – like living water.

Are these mental processes simply the internal workings of a mechanical mind? To me they are more like a mind bordering on the *Boundaries* of the transcendental.

4.7 A Prayer

This next experience could well have been a *Boundary* experience. On the other hand it could well have been something more profound – a *Transcendental* experience. Perhaps you should decide for yourself.

For this example we will have to travel back to that hillside cottage at Cefn-y-Crib that Jeanette and I had spent many years renovating.

The year, 1979, was significant, for both Jeanette's sister, Rosemary, and her father had died. From here on things in our little Garden of Eden took a steep dive for the worse. New people moved into the next farm, bringing with them their twenty-eight-year-old son who was attracted to schoolgirls. Someone close to me soon became ensnared by his good looks and childlike charms. I felt completely vulnerable, for I knew that it would end in grief for such a vulnerable young person. This helpless torment of mine seemingly had no solution. Having tried and retried every form of emotion and rationale I could think of I was completely at a loss. Utterly defeated, I finally resorted to prayer. It was the first time I can recall sincerely praying for personal help.

The most powerful answer to my prayer came when I was alone. Alone that is, except for my tears. 'What can I do?' was my repeated prayerful request. Then I heard an answer, 'Be available.' The voice was so vibrant, so clear, so near to me, that I looked about me, for I was sure that someone had come up behind me. There was no one there; yet I unequivocally heard, 'Be available.' A most perplexing message at the time, for I was then very much a person of action, I did not want to be told, in effect, to simply *wait*.

What was that voice?

Incidentally, I found then, and still find now, the message, 'Be available,' to be the most profound and the most difficult form of 'action' to take. To have to be passively aware, pained and filled with compassion, but helplessly 'waiting' is indeed hard. Like a father waiting for his prodigal son, I am still waiting.

These experiences, when in great humility the whole mind and consciousness are focused on a prayerful request which is given an uncharacteristic yet eminently practical solution, are perhaps on the very edge of being *Boundary* experiences. In these cases we are more likely to be entering into the *Transcendental* experience, where God is encountered.

These experiences, at the time, made me think again about the unexplained. I found, like so many other people, that stories of spontaneous human combustion, ghosts, supernatural powers of black magic, the devil or angels left me cold. They seemed to be explicable in terms of the evolutionary mind of man, science, psychology, hallucination, mass hysteria, drugs or the apparent randomness of life that we all seem to be subjected to. The more I rationalised, the less I could explain my own experience. It's all very well to say that drugs such as LSD will give visions, but I had not taken any drugs. It could have been my own mental stress causing electrochemical reactions that changed my brain patterns. But in the vast majority of cases, after the immediate effect of such induced experiences have worn off, there reappears a feeling of helplessness, depression, and a yearning to repeat the experience (by use of drugs or whatever). However, after an experience such as I am describing, there is a *permanent* feeling of wellbeing – even if one is a little perplexed.

While I agree that physiological effects that arise from stress may well account for many mental states, care is needed. When a solution to a desperate problem comes into the mind we must judge it with the test of time. Is it still appropriate one week, one month, one year, ten years later? Was it the sort of solution that your normal rational thinking would have deduced? If your answers are 'yes' for the former and 'no' for the latter then there is a very good chance that it is an experience of the sort I am trying to illustrate.

I have pondered long on the fact that it could be, for example, simply chemical or electromagnetic changes in the brain. But then the brain physiology is bound to change for rational thought to be produced at all!

What is the *initial* cause of these changes? Could it be a form of receiving system in the mind, sensitive to external phenomena? Could it be that an undetectable external stimulus initiated at least some of these changes? Is this human state in which we find ourselves a little more complex than the tangible earth on which we daily tread?

Can external phenomena be picked up 'directly' by a resonating, tuned mind? For me, experiences like the one I am about to share with you makes me truly believe that it can.

4.8 Prophecy or Pre-knowledge

Now to illustrate a true experience which can be most difficult to explain using only conventional science. This is the *Transcendental* experience.

Many years ago I was teaching mathematics in Saint Alban's RC Secondary School situated in Pontypool Park. During the mid-morning break I fell into conversation with a young English teacher who had, a few days previously, returned from a trip to India. She told me that a certain Sai Baba was claiming to be many things, including a reincarnation of Christ – she had been present when he had produced objects out of thin air.

My interest was naturally aroused. She was a level-headed, intellectual English teacher whom I had never expected to be so gullible. Her attitude to her experience was definitely out of character. I muttered that such a person would have to perform a personal miracle to get my support – such as improving my life-long hearing deficiency.

The next day she came up to me and handed me a book, which I looked at with mild interest as I had momentarily forgotten about our previous conversation. On the cover of the book was a large photo of a man in a long orange robe.

'Oh', I said, smiling. 'That's the book you showed me yesterday.'

The look on her face turned to one of surprise. 'No. I've never brought this book to school before.'

At first I thought that she was joking, but she was adamant and we concluded that I must have seen it elsewhere. This left me a little puzzled, as the memory of seeing it was so very fresh.

Bells and lessons interrupted us. That evening, when I arrived home, there was a letter asking me to attend hospital for an operation that was designed to improve my hearing. Suddenly I recalled the conversation of the day before in the morning coffee break and, in a flash, I remembered where I had seen the cover of the book before. It was the previous night – just as I was dropping off to sleep a completely clear picture of the orange-robed person on the front cover of that book had appeared to me – it was Sai Baba!

I cannot account for my preview of the book cover in any rational way. The initial 'mental' picture was so very clear. The time between my mental picture and seeing the book was less than a day. Now, my doubts of the psychic powers of Sai Baba still remain. Nevertheless the experience of clearly seeing his picture 'in my mind', the night before I had even seen the book itself, is beyond all doubt – and so detailed as to be beyond random chance.

By the way, that operation did improve my hearing!

Mystical experience has come to be viewed as an altered state of consciousness. It has been explained away in so many ways: a profound insight; a form of transiency and passivity; a losing touch with reality; a disturbed sense of time; a greater likelihood of experiencing emotional extremes; perceptual distortions; a sense of the ineffable; feelings of rejuvenation; hyper-suggestibility. Especially the latter, where the individual is more likely to accept statements or suggestions uncritically and thus is susceptible to many misinterpretations.

In no way do I recall having any of these feelings before recognising the cover of that book! The only emotion that I had at the time was one of bemused scepticism! I can think of no other explanation for this occurrence than it being from a transcendental cause.

4.9 Touching the Infinite

This is to be my last example.

My own introduction to the reality of God occurred when I was just three years old. It was a *Transcendental* experience.

It was in a wartime hospital in 1942. All my life I have remembered many of the experiences in that hospital with great clarity but, until recently, I have never talked openly about them.

It started shortly after my birthday when my mother had learned that I would have to go to hospital for what was then the serious operation of mastoidectomy (an ear operation involving the mastoid bone).

Many years later she told me that I had had more chance of dying than surviving all the necessary operations and she felt deeply responsible for my illness. This latter emotion was one of the hazards she faced in being such a good mother, one who would always wish to have done more.

I had been ill for some time. I did not seem to be fully conscious. It was almost like being an observer when I was put gently into a large barred cot. It was in an unfamiliar room leading off a very long corridor.

As she touched me with her soft loving hand, I felt that whatever was going to happen to me would be all right; my mother was there, standing close, caring, waiting to comfort me.

Suddenly I felt a chill run through my body, a growing concern, a feeling of being unsure, something I had not experienced ever before in my early years. There was something dreadful about to happen to me.

'You are not going to leave me are you, Mummy?'

'No, I'll never leave you,' she said, as she tried to come closer to me, but she turned away, and disappeared. My world died.

It must have been a few days later, I was much more active, and only wanted to go home. It was then that I had this vivid and very real experience.

I was standing in my pyjamas, as always in the hospital ward, when I saw that the door into the corridor was open. I cautiously looked around the door into a long corridor. The corridor seemed to attract me and I started walking down its long dimly lit length. It was a huge corridor that disappeared into murky darkness. There were doors everywhere. I walked on and on.

I would get away!

I wanted my life back. I wanted the warmth and love of my mother, who always knew my needs before I seemed to. I wanted to go back to my home.

Then I became aware that the corridor had changed. I had walked into a room and was standing in the middle of it. The corridor was behind me. I turned slowly around to my right, seeing all the room. I had walked to the end of the corridor. I was in a space. I recognised it. The space before the outside.

I remembered a little of the outside, a long hill – then nothing – then my home. What was in between? I could not recall. As I turned slowly around my eyes seemed to be getting bigger, as everything was becoming clearer and clearer. The room came into a sharp focus. I was fully alert. I could sense everything. There was no one about. My heightened awareness told me that there was no one in the rooms near by. And now I was facing, just across the room, a miracle – the two huge doors, each with a round blank eye looking down at me.

'That's where I came in!' I shouted. I ran joyfully to the doors. This would be my freedom, this is my desire. I will be away from here. I pushed.

The doors, three times my height, simply smiled down on me.

'I will open you,' I muttered under my breath, and pushed with all my might. Then at last I could feel movement. Yes, I could feel the doors move. I had won!

But, no, what is this? It was not the doors that were moving. It was me! I was moving, the floor beneath me was moving, as my feet slid from the great doors. The doors quietly smiled, their triumphant, unattached smile.

I am angry. I am screaming at the doors, my hands spread above me, pressed hard against the immobile, unfeeling, doors. My fingers are taut and straining to get away from each other.

I push, I scream, I shout, I cry, I loose my all in overwhelming agony.

The doors smile down.

I cannot stand it, I scream and scream and shout and push and surrender myself within the horror of my own internal fire. I am consumed with temper. I will destroy all. I do not care. I hate, hate, hate.

Then suddenly, without any warning, without introduction, without my knowing, and without a sound, I am leaving the little boy, which is me. I look down and see the hands, the arms, the room. My understanding seems to touch the infinite, as I am made fully aware of the impossibility of the little boy. I feel warm love emanating from the universe in which I am suspended.

I am back in myself. I am calm. I am knowing. I am love. I am accepting. I am blessed. I start to walk back.

A caring hand reaches out from beneath a friendly face. I was only dimly aware of being talked to, for I was at peace.

Today I am still grateful for whatever held the hand of my 'three-year-old' spirit, before that kindly nurse gave me her hand to hold.

Of course these early years of one's life could be full of many types of mental quirks and dreams. Nevertheless, when revisiting the Pontypool and District Hospital in later years, the doors with the circular windows, the reception hall, which I originally thought was a room, and the long corridor were all there. Even the room in the hospital in which I was first placed in a cot was confirmed as the one from my early memories, although at the time of my enquiries it was used for something completely different.

There are so many other things that I remember of that hospital. Parents were considered a hazard and therefore not allowed to see their children very often, so my father would scramble down the steep bank at the side of the ward to give me pennies to play with. Being given pieces of chocolate for not crying when the blood-soaked lengths of linen were pulled out from the hole behind my right ear. Christmas, the sharing days. Being with, and admiring, a very beautiful nurse in a lift that was stuck between floors.

Never in my whole stay at the hospital, after that early experience, did I feel any real fear. I expect that the five operations during those 12 months in hospital brought on tears at times but I have no recollection of any pain or even of discomfort.

Perhaps it was the kindly nurse coming for me and helping me, but I do not think so now, and I never have thought so. Unlike many childhood memories this one cannot have been formed from photographs or by the helpful comments of others and my experiences of the world were quite limited at the time.

Was my hospital experience simply a mental quirk that helped me through difficulties? There is no simple answer. I am sure that if my mental state had been monitored at the time it could have indicated that I was suffering from an illusion for I strongly suspect that there was no tangible presence. But then, as I was aware

of something, my brain would naturally respond to that awareness, for how else could I know of its existence? But any measured
brain response cannot even begin to show the true origin of such
experience.

I am also conscious that the passage of time can distort memory, and over time when we cannot remember what happened we
invent, or confabulate, up to five per cent of the missing information. However, the unchanging nature of this memory and its clarity has always been very profound and bears no resemblance to
any other childhood memory.

4.10 Assessing Transcendental Experiences

Transcendental experiences are given many natural and rational explanations by psychoanalysts and social scientists. These explanations include: altered states brought about by increased external stimulation and/or motor activity or emotion, e.g. ecstatic trances, religious conversions during revival meetings and amnesia; altered states brought about by reduced external stimulation and/or motor activity, e.g. dreaming, somnambulism, hypnagogic and hypnopompic sleep and states brought about by sensory deprivation; altered states brought about by increased alertness or mental involvement, e.g. prolonged observation of a radar screen or fervent praying; altered states brought about by decreased alertness or relaxation, e.g. daydreaming, meditation states, mediumistic trances or deep relaxation; altered states brought about by physical factors, which may be spontaneous, or as a result of fasting. Then there are known changes due to dehydration, hyperventilation, temporal lobe seizures, drug effects and drug-withdrawal effects.

These classifications definitely describe some of our human experience, but for many people they represent an over-simplification, and ignore the pivotal point in understanding that of *being*.

The only possible sign of someone, other than ourselves, having a transcendental experience is that it will change the priorities of their life. Perhaps it is as Jesus is reported to have told us in the Gospel of Matthew (7:16), 'You will recognise them by their fruits.' But, even the 'proof' of a 'changed lifestyle' will never be absolutely conclusive of their sincerity. Other people's claims are like a minefield, where experiences can be misused and become lost in the excesses of a particular brand of religious or secular belief.

Today it is not unusual to hear of clairvoyants, spiritualists and purveyors of such pseudo-science as 'crystal power' having all sorts of speculative theories. I have, for example, heard it suggested that an 'out of body experience' is,

a fully conscious and functional energetic echo which reflects into an astral body and is then maintained outside the bounds of the physical body by a subtle energy-connecting linkage known as the Silver Cord.

To me these statements represent interesting possibilities, but they are much more likely to be speculative fantasies.

There are many who prey on our natural fears, our longing for stability, our desire to know the future or to find a cure for mental or physical pain. Do ancient Jewish Qabalah translators, modern astrologers and tarot card readers report all their failures as well as their successes? Their inclusive language, tempered with charisma and empathy, is amazingly convincing. I sometimes wonder if they are simply making an interesting focus for their own lives?

Even in our deceptive world, there are still people who walk with humility among the poor and needy, and in so doing point to being guided by a reality which may well be transcendental in origin, such as the late Mother Teresa of Calcutta, Brother Roger Schutz-Marsauche of Taize, Jean Vanier of L'Arche communities and many, many more.

The source, or origin, of the experiences that I have illustrated in this chapter may always prove to be undetectable by conventional science. But one thing is for sure, they are all part of the normal process of being fully human. Some of these experiences point to a reality that I believe transcends external worldly events. I conclude the following, therefore. The first three examples concerning innovation and inspiration in the form of 'examination techniques', 'aircraft black box design' and that 'river swan inspiring ideas about God' are all *Normal* experiences. I believe that they are most likely to be confined to the electrochemical functioning of the brain, limited by sensory experience and genetic make-up.

The last two examples, of 'seeing a book cover in my mind before the event' and 'my experience as a three-year-old child in hospital', were illustrations of *Transcendental* experiences concerned with 'pre-knowledge' and 'touching the infinite'. These experiences do not sit easily within the classifications of the psychoanalyst. The sceptic could explain them as the mind changing the evidence itself, a form of modified memory. In some instances this could be true, but not in these two cases. Particularly in the first case, where explanations that include modified memory would seem to be falsifying the evidence in order to make non-transcendental theories appear to be the only sensible explanations for identifying a book before ever coming into contact with it. I am left with no doubt that the experience was of a transcendental nature that required more than brain/mind interaction. There was no stress, no prayer, no drugs. The vision in the hospital brought about a permanent and a sustained understanding. These two experiences appear to be far removed from 'defects' of the mechanism of the brain-mind.

Between these two categories are the *Boundary* experiences. These are the experiences that may be of a transcendental, visionary form or the natural workings of the complex mind. They are the *Boundary* experiences between the worldly and the transcendental, typified by the experiences cited above, which concern 'seeing God as a teenager', 'the Church on the hill', and 'my prayer answered'. These experiences are the limiting or the *Boundary* conditions, as they may or may not contain transcendental facets. Personally, I believe that they also contained aspects that were of a transcendental nature, especially the 'Be available' answer to my prayer.

Transcendental experiences do occur. Perhaps we should not be unduly surprised if some people have no recollection of transcendental experiences for, after all, is everyone a born mathematician, a great artist or able to converse fluently in 15 languages? There is no doubt that the mind can be affected by drugs, it can be physically, chemically or electrically defective. Nevertheless, there are states of mind which undoubtedly point to a transcendental reality which itself points to the immanence of an 'Ultimate' – which I am calling God.

But again it is worth stressing that the case studies used in this chapter are only to illustrate the possible modes of the human mind that border on the transcendental. It is your own experiences that truly count.

Chapter 5

Aspects of God

The human race has accumulated countless aspects of the god phenomenon. This chapter introduces but three. The 'Personal', the 'Pointers' and the 'Possible'.

5.1 Personal - The Gift of Life

Life sometimes seems like a roller-coaster. For me it has moments of deep empathy, sublime joy and great excitement peppered with pain, meaninglessness and depression. However, life in all its forms is a gift.

Several years ago I was outside Llandaff Cathedral in Cardiff when, for a brief moment, I became mesmerised by a stone that had been discarded from the Jasper Tower renovations. It struck me that although that stone had many characteristics they did not include sensitivity, emotion, intelligence, love, understanding and consciousness - at least not that I could relate to. It was devoid of the 'gift of life'. And I realised that even in my lowest state, I have, and I am, much more than the stone. At that moment I knew that it was *by using a stone as the datum that I could begin to measure my gift of life!*

Using such a measure as a stone, it was apparent that no matter what ills befall me, even in that last instant before my death, I will still be more than the stone, and *the more is the gift of life.*

From Chapter 2 it was apparent that all of existence exudes reason and purpose, has logic, has shape, has pattern. What then can be the reason for the existence of an imperfect person such as myself? If I decide that any creator of 'me' has simple objectives like making me rich or handsome, or successful in such things as sport, politics, commerce and so on, then all I see of the human condition does not make sense.

Although there is a sort of immortality in passing on our ideas, artefacts, skills and emoluments to the next generation, whatever contribution one makes to the advancement of mankind, it will be nothing in, say, ten million years time. All earthly success will disappear like the tide-battered sandcastles on the shore of a restless sea.

Our own inevitable death points unequivocally to the fact that the purpose of life cannot be the accumulation of wealth and possessions, in fact it cannot be any form of physical or mental perfection. It is relatively easy to think of worldly attributes that are beyond even the most perfect human being. For example, who can fly unaided as well as a lowly dung beetle, let alone a swift or swallow.

So, I reason that our existence cannot be to perfect anything physical, artistic or academic for eventually all fade away. Perhaps what matters for our inner development is not the actual pain or pleasure of life, but how we respond to that pain or pleasure. It is often mishaps in our lives that enhance our desirable characteristics, such as patience, understanding and acceptance.

Thus if my *being* has purpose in itself so must the creator of that *being* have purpose. It seems rational then that whatever gave me the gift of life 'beyond the stone', has allowed me:

to appreciate the natural beauty of hills, rivers and woods;
to feel the warmth of a summer evening;
to resonate with the music and poetry;
to taste the bitter sweetness of earthly love;
to become more aware that I am;

to move from the life of doing to the life of being;

to be given more than I need to survive, that I may reap the pleasure of giving to others;

to suffer pain and loss and be slowly drawn forward to a deeper understanding.

To understand the gift of each of our individual lives, we should not be considering owning surplus possessions or aiming for some theoretical human perfection, but we should start by taking into account the 'life', or should I say the non-life, of the stone. Look to the stone, not to perfection, to start the journey of understanding. For after all what can anyone claim to have achieved to deserve any gift at all, let alone one as precious as *life* itself?

I have come to believe that although I try to avoid all forms of suffering and pain, it can be, and often is, an opportunity. For I find that I am in complete agreement with the words of the late theologian David Watson who, when dying of cancer, wrote, 'The primary question to ask is not "why" but "what" – Lord, what are you saying in this?'

For example, was the terrorist attack on the World Trade Centre on the 11th of September 2001 the work of an evil force, or was it a 'wake up call' from God in this age of globalisation? Surely we should be always asking *what* are we learning from life's harsh blows as well as enjoying the good times.

In the last analysis, I believe that we have been given a gift – a gift of an impermanent nature perhaps, but it is a gift, the gift of *life itself*. The fact that the reason for the gift is unfathomable does not detract from our personal existence being a *gift*.

Why some people (and animals?) are unable to comprehend a meaning for their lives, while others of us are given insights beyond the physical envelope of life, I cannot begin to answer. Maybe we cannot easily understand God's purpose because, as mortals, we think in terms of rewards, aims, goals and meanings that are limited by our worldly understanding and experience. We should not expect that in our human ignorance we could begin to comprehend the full wisdom of God. Could anyone explain the theory of relativity to a pet hamster or the joy of sex to an undeveloped foetus? Perhaps we are in a human state to develop our faith in, not necessarily our knowledge of, God.

5.2 Common Pointers to the Existence of God

The world is filled with pointers; perhaps it is nothing but pointers. How we understand these pointers does, to a large extent,
depend upon our worldview. Pointers for some are such that they
are sufficient proof that an omnipotent creator exists.

Next time you are about to pull up a garden weed, stop for a
moment.

I was at my sister's holiday house in the French Dordogne in
the July of 1997 when I became aware of a small patch of weeds. I
found myself looking with great care at just one tiny, blue flower.
Time stood still. The flower became newborn in my sight - so frag-
ile, so soft, so delicate with its myriad of interlacing blues and
whites.

My empathy struggled to link with the essence of the flower.
Looking deeply into the flower's beauty I felt overwhelming awe.
My awe spread out – increasing, as I became aware of a knowing
beyond the limits of my five senses. I felt with my whole being. I
felt the boundary of incandescent blue balanced on the greenness
of the plant; how the plant was attached to the ground; how the
ground contacted other plants; how the ground was under and
holding me – as it is holding you now.

Later, my sister Joan, thinking I wished to know the name of my
little flower, kindly told me that it was the common germander
speedwell.

Are the 'common' things that surround us every day the true
miracles that point to the reality of God?

Then again, could it simply be that life is like the beautifully intricate and temporary sand 'paintings' of some Buddhist monks? For it seems to me that maximum rewards come to us *during* our actions, not from the 'permanency' of their results.

Many great beacons of light have guided mankind towards a civilised way of living by encouraging the longing that seems to already exist within the human heart.

Why should it be so?

Why do people rally around the good, help their neighbour, love and see beauty in nature, stand awe-struck at the great music of the cosmos or the fathomless wonder of the quantum world?

Why the inner glow waiting to be fanned into the flame which seeks perfection?

Why should mankind have a concept of perfection? For all of nature by its very limited 'life' form, exudes imperfection and compromise.

The spectrum of humanity is wide, from the selfishness eloquently portrayed by Darwin, to the altruistic love so clearly depicted by the life and sacrifice of Jesus of Nazareth. These characteristics are within us all – they are intrinsic in our being human. We can choose which of our inner voices we allow to dominate our thoughts, our words and our very actions in life.

We seem to vibrate with the rhythm of life and yet be separate from it. We create poetry, art and music, which are separate from us and yet at times seem to resonate with our very essence.

Who can sit silently for an hour or so in a Sikh temple, a gurdwara, and listen to the sincere singing rhythmical praises of the Wonderful Lord, 'Waheguru, Waheguru, Waheguru', without feeling something beyond being simply the summation of a mass of cells?

Who can stay with Cistercian monks for a long summer's day and listen to their seven periods of Gregorian chant, starting at dawn and finishing at dusk, without sensing more to life than the physical world?

The tinkle of a Ramakrishna Arti bell can fill me with awe; even so it is not in itself the proof of any reality within the god phenomenon.

All these rhythms which strike and enhance our inner chords can give us true imageless thoughts and are some of the great experiences in which the human race can, and does, share. Perhaps this shared capacity offers us some clues concerning our search for authenticating the reality of God. For open-hearted fellowship through unspoken thoughts has aspects that are universal.

Are the tears of compassion flowing from a truly altruistic person to be viewed as only mechanisms that have evolved as necessary ingredients for group survival? Are we following our inclinations, like a pack of wild dogs, where individuals are believed to 'instinctively' sacrifice themselves for the sake of the pack? Superficially the answer could well be yes! But look a little deeper and we find that in humans altruism is not so simplistic. From the sacrifice of millions fighting for an ideal to the soldier who carries a dying man across a battlefield, all such actions reduce each individual's chances of survival (and, incidentally, any subsequent preservation of their own unique genetic pattern).

Sri Guru Teg Bahadur Ji, the Ninth Guru of the Sikh movement in the Punjab back in 1675 freely allowed himself to be taken prisoner and knowingly suffered a slow and agonising death in a bid to convince the world that each man should be free to choose his own religious path.

There is the better-known example of the immeasurable compassion of the founder of Christianity, Jesus, who sacrificed his life so that all may come to realise God.

Then there are the completely altruistic motivations of those who follow the teachings of the Bodhisattva. A Buddhist's way of life, many thousands of years old, demonstrates that true unselfish compassion wells up from the very core of some individuals. One can point to exceptions within such a fraternity, but the vast majority of those who study the Bodhicitta to take the Bodhisattva Vow are simply struggling to increase their ability to help others through further development of their own natural compassion. They are moved by the mind and its great compassion that turns itself towards beings and thinks, 'I must liberate all beings from suffering...' It is a thought only of love and concern, far removed from 'Nature red in tooth and claw'.

Even if there were some psychological development in mankind's evolution that produced true altruism, surely the most logical explanation for it would be that it emanates from the intelligence behind existence itself. Naturally it is simple to think of theories which relate altruism to blind evolution. But such theories conveniently leave out so many unresolved factors – from the puzzle of finding places of great danger, such as snow-capped mountains, beautiful and enchanting, through the enigma of human tears, to the reality of *being* itself.

5.3 Possible attributes of God

We will finish with a cursory look at some possible attributes of God as developed through the wisdom of world scriptures.

As we have discussed, the only unshakeable basis for the verification of God is through the personal understanding and experience of *being*, when one begins to experience what I have called 'the breath of God'. When I need a rock of unshakeable 'proof' for my belief in the transcendental reality, I return to simply just *being*. It is then that I become sure beyond debates, arguments and logic, sure beyond history, sure beyond prophets, seers, shamans or gurus, sure beyond scripture, sure beyond miracles, and sure beyond science – I *know* that life has meaning, I am relevant to that meaning and something gave me the gift of life. That something I am calling God.

To return to the possible attributes of God: down the ages we humans have attempted to define the characteristics of God. Perhaps the most profound definitions are to be found in Hindu scriptures. My initial foray into this vast collection led me to the understanding that they are the largest and contain the oldest concepts of the god phenomenon that the world has ever known. Vedanta is the philosophy evolved from the teachings of a collection of ancient Indian scriptures known as the Vedas, and contains literature that is still being written today.

It does not owe its origin to any one person or prophet. Vedanta presents an all-embracing view of existence. This view, which is described in meticulous detail, has evolved from speculations, experiences and analysis of the ancient seers and rishis who were responsible for its development.

These ancient ones found that, in the external world, no search would give the answer to their questions so they turned to an examination of the inner world, the precincts of the mind. By this means they found that they were able to penetrate the veil obscuring the truth they sought, and found the external to be but a dull reflection of the internal.

Vedanta means 'the end' or 'the essence'. It is the concluding portion of the Vedas with particular reference to the set of scriptures known as the Upanishads. The principles of the Vedanta are twofold:

1. Each soul is potentially divine. (Man in his true nature is divine Spirit, identical with the inmost being and reality of the universe.)
2. The goal of life is to manifest this divinity. (The differences between man and man are only the differences in the degree to which the divinity within is manifest... This divine nature can be gradually uncovered, known and entered into by means of prayer, meditation and the living of a disciplined life – a life that seeks to overcome the obstacles of desire, fear, hatred, possessiveness, vanity and pride... If you harm anyone, you harm yourself. If you help anyone, you help yourself. All feelings of separateness, exclusiveness, intolerance and hatred are not only 'wrong', they are the blackest ignorance, because they deny the Omnipresent Divinity.)

Within the great diversity of Indian beliefs there is a definition of the inner God, the Atman, a universal aspect of which is Brahman.

Brahman is the Absolute, the Supreme Reality of Non-dualistic Vedanta. Brahman is the macrocosm, or totality, of souls. Brahman, sometimes referred to as the Supreme Brahman, is One.

Atman is the individual soul, pure Brahman, Consciousness. Atman has no body, but is the spark of divinity that resides in each human heart.

To help human understanding and communication the

Vedanta tells of Brahman having an attributable part, and an attributeless or unknowable part (beyond all human understanding). The attributable part (the Cosmic God) is called Saguna Brahman, which has qualities that we humans can relate to. The attributeless or unknowable part is referred to as Nirvana Brahman.

Today East and West meet on the idea that God is One and agree that the totality of God is above and beyond all human understanding of space, time and energy, while also acknowledging that under certain conditions God seems be part of our mundane daily lives.

It is to the knowable aspects of God that we must surely turn first if we are to progress in our understanding of God. This will set us on a course of action, which will, in the end, take us towards the attributeless or 'unknowable' aspects of God.

Perhaps humanity has been given the highest form of the cosmic or knowable part of God in the form of Jesus. Jesus could well be the knowable aspect of God that brings a universal message to mankind. He may even be the *ultimate human manifestation of God*, a pointer towards the reality of God that helps us to break away from our own ego, and realise our need for complete humility before such awesome creativeness.

I believe that God is leading us to look outwards at the world and engage with it. To walk in faith, love and fellowship with all we meet.

The stained glass east window of Saint Edmund's Church in my chosen home town of Crickhowell gives a clear illustration of God as acclaimed by many people in the West.

On the left windowpane there is a lamb depicting the 'knowable' God in the form of the life and ultimate sacrifice of Jesus. The right windowpane shows a dove – representing peace, 'the peace beyond all understanding'. It symbolizes the Holy Spirit through which communication with God is possible. In the top pane of glass is a simple star to indicate the limitlessness of God.

For me, all three are aspects of God which I can understand and relate to.

Chapter 6
Conclusions

To me, it seems an unbelievable lack of humility that allows some to think that they are, or are about to become, masters of all the knowledge concerning the creation of our universe. They appear to have such overwhelming egos that they come to believe that their knowledge, wisdom, physical prowess and material gifts are *solely* due to themselves: their breeding, intelligence, strength, hard work or whatever. They do not begin to acknowledge their own cosmic insignificance.

They fail to recognise that there are many unsolved mysteries in life, the most profound being our very existence, *being*, and the creation of that existence.

In fact, all our tomorrows contain mysteries, puzzles around which our minds form questions. There are trivial questions such as what clothes or shoes to wear. There are questions that are answered by science, engineering and mathematics. Then there are the more profound questions, such as the origin of life, the functioning of the quanta world or the secrets of the cosmos – questions that have human answers anchored to facts by the thinnest of threads. But all these questions are small, even insignificant, when they are compared with the 'Big Question' – does God exist? For such a question contains within it the mystery of our own origin, identity, relevance, suffering and inevitable death.

In journeying through the writing of this book I have tried to show that experience is the common element for both conventional science and the science of God.

When we turned our attention to science, technology and mathematics I hope it became clear that the knowledge available in these disciplines is a bottomless pit of information with no sign of any bedrock of absolute truth for the meaning of our lives. By considering individual realities it became apparent that human understanding surpasses science; for conventional science, by its empirical nature, sets artificial boundaries to understanding. The boundaries of science stop at the edges of the phenomenal world with the inevitable result of excluding the transcendental. Thus science, engineering and mathematics in their present form will never prove or disprove the reality of something that allows 'me' personally to exist.

Scientists, and others, who eliminate the transcendental at the onset are like James Challis, that nineteenth-century professor of astronomy at Cambridge who was convinced that he never saw Neptune – yet his own notes later revealed that he had seen it!

It has become clear that some people appear to have a deeper understanding of the existence of God than do others. This should come as no surprise for like any human talent it may be naturally present in one individual while, for another, such understanding will be a long and often painful process to achieve. Knowing that God exists is certainly not related to such earthly attributes as intellect, intelligence or birthright. There are, however, pointers to the truth of other people's reported transcendental experiences. I believe that if a person who claims to have had a transcendental experience does not show a very low attachment to worldly possessions and pleasures, then their 'visions' or 'visitations' of God are the imagination of a fertile mind. For the mind can so easily produce self-deception. The more we progress God-wards, the less significant our earthly treasures and passing pleasures become and the more we dwell at the null-point of true peace of mind.

I have taken great care not to jump to conclusions when presenting my case studies containing experiences that point beyond the physical manifestation of our human condition to the transcendental reality. Discovering God is not concerned with conventional science nor with the more universal descriptors of mathematics. The bedrock of truth is only verified by experience – that is the personal experience of a sincere seeker of truth who, when all alone and *with the deepest humility*, realises *being* and becomes profoundly aware of 'the breath of God'.

Realising *being* is probably one of the most difficult things to achieve in this life, for life experiences themselves move us on with such speed that, all too often, we do not have time to grasp and to ponder our more profound experiences. It is a paradox, for it is the experience of life that can allow us to receive the pulse of inner understanding. Yet if we do not stop at that point, it is life that robs us of the chance to assimilate any possible transcendental meaning.

How do we know when we have achieved this inner understanding? In fact, we will *know*, for *inner understanding brings emotions of deep sorrow for the suffering of other people, and great joy for our own enlightenment.*

It is by the patient exploration of our own personal existence, along with the heartfelt desire to experience the transcendental, that we may arrive on the first rung of 'the ladder of transcendental realisation'. This first rung is the unshakeable knowledge that a transcendental reality exists and inextricably points to the reality of 'God'.

There is an experiment that is beyond science, beyond art and music, beyond the messages of the great prophets, gurus, seers and men filled with God, beyond the wisdom of the scriptures and the company of the saints. The experiment that reveals the transcendental part of our human condition is within everyone's grasp. 'Ask, and you will receive; seek, and you will find; knock, and the door will be opened to you.' (Gospel of Matthew 7:7) There is no quick fix, no simple guide to understanding transcendental reality. Transcendental knowledge cannot be learned, only experienced and verified by an open-minded search for truth.

To sail on the sea of true transcendental understanding is a gift of God beyond all others. Once experienced it will be enhanced by prayer, meditation, scriptural readings and the company of righteous people.

Further Reading

Scriptural

Holy Bible, King James (1611) Version. Printed at the Oxford University Press London: Henry Frowde.

The Revised English Bible with the Apocrypha. Oxford University Press; Cambridge University Press 1989.

The New Jerusalem Bible. Darton, Longman & Todd Ltd 18th June 1985.

Holy Bible, New Revised Standard Version Anglicised Edition. Oxford University Press 1995. ISBN 0191070009.

Sri Guru Granth Sahib. Translated by **Manmohan Singh**. Shiromani Gurdwara Parbandhak Committee Amritsar. Third Edition:
>Volume 1 Pages 1 to 150. Printed 1987.
>Volume 2 Pages 151 to 346. Printed 1988.
>Volume 3 Pages 347 to 536. Printed 1989.
>Volume 4 Pages 537 to 727. Printed 1989.
>Volume 5 Pages 728 to 875. Printed 1990.
>Volume 6 Pages 876 to 1106. Printed 1991.
>Volume 7 Pages 1107 to 1293. Printed 1992.
>Volume 8 Pages 1294 to 1430. Printed 1992.

The Holy Qur'an. King Fahd Holy Qur'an Printing Complex, according to the Royal decree number 12412, dated 27.10.1405 AH.

The Upanishads. **Swami Nikhilananda**. Publisher Ramakrishna-Vivekananda Centre, New York.
>Volume 1 containing: Katha, Isa, Kena, and Mundaka Upanishads.
>Fifth edition 1990.
>Volume 2 containing: Svetasvatara, Prasna, and Mandukya Upanishads, also Gaudapada's Karika. Third Edition 1990.
>Volume 3 containing: Aitareya and Bribadaranyaka Upanishads.
>Third edition 1990.
>Volume 4 containing: Taittiriya and Chhandogya Upanishads.
>Second edition 1979.

Bhagavad-Gita (complete edition). **A C Bhaktivedanta Swami Parbhupada**. The Bhaktivedanta Book trust. Seventh Printing 1993.

The Dhammapada. The sayings of the Buddha. **Thomas Byrom**. Shambhala

Boston and London 1993.

The Gospel of Sri Ramakrishna. Seventh Printing 1984. Printed by Ramakrishna - Vivekananda Centre. New York, ISBN 0-911206-01-9.

Bodhisattvacharyavatara (A Guide to the Bodhisattva's Way of Life). Translated by **Stephen Batchelor**. Sixth reprint 1993. Published by the Library of Tibetan Works and Archives. Dharamsala. ISBN 8185102597.

The Gospel of Zarathushtra. **Duncan Greenlees**. The Theosophical Pubs. House India 1951.

General

1. **Abhishiktananda**. *Saccidananda - A Christian approach to Advaitic Experience*. (1990) ISPCK.

2. **Alford, E Alan**. *God of the New Millennium*. (1997) Hodder and Stoughton.

3. **Aitken, E H**. *The Five Windows of the Soul - thoughts on perceiving*. (1898) John Murray, Albemarle Street London.

4. **Balado, J L Gonzalez**. *The Story of Taize*. (1991) Mowbray ISBN 0264671708.

5. **Barbour, Ian G**. (Professor, Dep. of Religion). *Three Paths from Nature to Religious Belief and Science, God and Nature*. (1995) The Idreos Lectures Manchester College Oxford. ISBN 0950871567.

6. **Binney, James and Merrifield, Michael**. *Galactic Astronomy*. (1998) Princeton University Press. ISBN 0691025657.

7. **Blue, Rabbi**. *My Affair with Christianity*. (1998) Hodder and Stoughton.

8. **Bowden, John**. *Jesus – the unanswered questions*. (1988) SMC Press ISBN 0334020999.

9. **Caritas, Veritas Maxima**. *The Mystery of Miracles*. (1978) Kegan Paul & Co. 1 Paternoster Square.

10. **Casti, John L**. *Paradigms Lost - images of man in the mirror of science*. (1990) Scribners, Macdonald. ISBN 0356187977.

11. **Cottingham, John**. *Western Philosophy - an anthology*. (1996) Blackwell Publishers Ltd. ISBN 0631186271.

12. **Crook, John H**. *The Evolution of Human Consciousness.* (1980) Oxford University Press. ISBN 0198571747.

13. **Davies, Paul**. *The Mind of God - a synthesis of science, philosophy and theology.* (1993) Touchstone Books. ISBN 0671797182.

14. **Durrant, A**. *Quantum Physics of Matter.* (2000) Institute of Physics Publishing and Open University. ISBN 0750307218.

15. **Evans, David S**. *The Eddington Enigma.* (1999) Xlibris. ISBN 0738801313.

16. **Faivre, Bro**. *Daniel. Prayer of People of Faith.* (1994.) Westminster Interfaith.

17. **Fox, Matthew**. *The Coming of the Cosmic Christ.* (1983) Harper & Row. ISBN 0060629150

18. **France, R T**. *Jesus The Radical.* (1989) Inter-Varsity Press. ISBN 085110844X.

19. **Fry**. *The Emergence of Life on Earth.* (2000) Free Association Books. ISBN 1853434817.

20. **Goldberg, Jeff**. *Anatomy of a Scientific Discovery - the race to discover the secret of human pain and pleasure.* (1989) Bantam Books ISBN 0553176161.

21. **Goleman, D and Thurman, A F** (eds). **Gyatso, Tenzin** (the fourteenth Dalai Lama); **Benson, Herbert; Thurman, Robert; Gardner, Howard; Goleman, Daniel and other participants** (authors). *MindScience - an East-West dialogue.* 1991. The Harvard Mind Science Symposium. Wisdom Publications Boston. ISBN 0861710065.

22. **Gribbin, John**. *Companion to the Cosmos.* (1996) Wiedenfeld & Nicolson. ISBN 0297817256.

23. **Grof, Stanislav**. *Realms of the Human Unconscious -observations from LSD research.* (1993) Souvenir Press. ISBN 0285648829.

24. **Halle, Louis J**. *Out of Chaos.* (1977) Houghton Miffin Co. Boston. ISBN 0395253578.

25. **Hawking, Stephen W**. *A Brief History of Time: from the big bang to black holes.* (1988) Bantam.

26. **Heidegger, Martin**. Translated by **John Macquarrie and Edward Robinson**. *Being and Time.* (1973) Oxford. Basil Blackwell ISBN 063210190X.

27. **Hobson, J Allan**. *The Chemistry of Conscious States.* Little and Brown.

28. **Howard, Michael**. *God in the Depths.* (1999) SPCK. ISBN 0218051720.

29. **Hoyle, Fred and Wickramasinghe, N Chandra.** *Diseases from Space.* (1979) Sphere Books. ISBN 0722147546 science.

30. **Huges, John** (trans.); **Jean-Didier, Vicent** (author). *The Biology of Emotions.* (1990) Basil Blackwell. ISBN 0631160736.

31. **Jackson, Mariette (ed).** *Egypt's Lost City.* (1999) A BBC product printed by InSpeed, Luton. ISBN 1861200463.

32. **Jones, Cheslyn; Wainwright Geoffrey; Yarnold, S J Edward** (eds.). *The Study of Spirituality.* (1996) SPCK. ISBN 0281041504.

33. **Jones, Steve.** *In the Blood - God, genes and destiny.* (1996) HarperCollins. ISBN 0002555115.

34. **Learner, Eric J.** *The Big Bang Never Happened - a startling refutation of the dominant theory of the origin of the universe.* (1992) Simon and Schuster Ltd. ISBN 0671711008.

35. **Leonard, George.** *The Silent Pulse.* (1979) Wildwood House Ltd. ISBN 0704503913.

36. **Leuba, James H.** *The Psychology of Religious Mysticism.* (1972) (first pub. 1925) Routledge & Kegan Paul Ltd. ISBN 0710073178.

37. **Levine, Stephen.** *Guided Meditations, Explorations and Healings.* (1993) Gateway Books, Bath. ISBN 0946551855.

38. **Levi, Primo.** *The Drowned and the Saved.* (1988) (origin German) Michael Joseph London published by Penguin Group. ISBN 0718130634. [R049]

39. **Macquarrie, John** and **Robinson, Edward** (trans. from German by **Martin Heidegger**). *Being and Time.* (1973) Oxford. Basil Blackwell. ISBN 063210190X.

40. **Marcel, Gabriel.** *The Mystery of Being - reflection and mystery Volume 1.* (1978) University Press of America. ISBN 0819133108.

41. **Matthews, Melvin.** *The Hidden Word.* (1993) Darton Longman and Todd Ltd. ISBN 0232519994.

42. **McGrath, Alister E.** *Science and Religion - an introduction.* (1999) Blackwell Publishing Ltd. ISBN 0631208429.

43. **Mills, Joy.** *The Mystery of Human Identity.* (1981) The Theosophical Society, London, booklet.

44. **Morange, Michael.** *The Misunderstood Gene.* Harvard University Press. ISBN 0674003365.

45. **Nikhilananda, Swami**. *Self Knowledge*. Published Sri Ramakrishna Math, Mylapore, madras 600 004. ISBN 8171203981.

46. **Peacocke, Arthur**. *Theology for a Scientific Age –(enlarged edition)*. (1993) SMC Press. ISBN 0334025478.

47. **Penrose, Roger**. *The Emporor's New Mind*. (1999) Oxford University Press. ISBN 0192861980.

48. **Penrose, Roger**. *The Large, the Small and the Human Mind*. (2000) Canto. ISBN 0521785723.

49. **Polkinghorne, Rev. Dr. John**. *Knowledge and Understanding*. (1999) SPCK. ISBN 0281052638.

50. **Polkinghorne, Rev. Dr. John**. *Science and Christian Belief - theological reflections of a bottom-up thinker*. (1997) University Press Cambridge. ISBN 0281047146.

51. **Rinpoche, Bokar**. *Taking the Bodhisattva Vow*. (1997) ClerPoint Press. ISBN 0963037188.

52. **Saha, N**. *The Complete Works of Swami Vivekananda*. (1984) Ashutosh Lithographic Co. India. Mayavati Memorial Edition Published by Swami Ananyananda President, Advaita Ashrama Mayavati.

53. **Satre, Jean-Paul**, translated by **Hazel E Barnes**. *Being and Nothingless - an essay in phenomenological ontology* (original 1943, English translation reprint 1998). ISBN 0415040299.

54. **Singh, Gopal**. *A History of the Sikh People*. 1469-1978. World University Press.

55. **Smith, Barbara**. *Truth, Liberty, Religion - essays celebrating two hundred years of Manchester College*. (1986) Manchester College Oxford. ISBN 0950871516.

56. **Smythe, Colin**. *The Book of Kells*. (1994) Trinity College, Dublin ISBN 0851052983.

57. **Stamp, Eleonore** and **Murray, Michael** (eds.). *Philosophy of Religion - the big question*. (1999) Blackwell Publishers Ltd. ISBN 0631206043.

58. **Sternberg Robert J**. *Wisdom - its nature, origins and development*. (1990) Cambridge University Press. ISBN 0521364531.

59. **Swindells, John** (Ed.). *A Human Search - Bede Griffiths reflects on his life*. (1979) Burns and Oats. ISBN 0860122743.

60. **Turvok, Neil**, (Ed.) *Dialogues in Cosmology*. (1996) World Scientific. ISBN 9810228600.

61. **Watson, David**. *Fear no Evil - a personal struggle with cancer*. (1984) Hodder and Stoughton. ISBN 0340346418.

62. **Wilber, Ken**. *The Spectrum of Consciousness*. (1977) Quest Books. ISBN 0835604934.

63. **Wilson, John**. *Language and the Pursuit of Truth*. (1980) Cambridge University Press. ISBN 0521068215.

64. **Wordsworth** Poetry Library, The. *The Works of William Wordsworth*. (1995) Wordsworth Editions Limited. ISBN 1853264016.

65. **Wright, Roger**. *Non Zero*. (2000) Little Brown and Co. ISBN 0316644854.

66. **Yatiswarananda, Swami**. *Meditation and Spiritual Life*. (1995) Nithyananda Printers Bagalore - 560 050.

Acknowledgements

I would like to thank all those who have given me permission to include extracts in this book, as indicated below.

Every effort has been made to trace and contact copyright owners. If there are any inadvertent omissions or error in the acknowledgements I apologize to those concerned and will remedy these in any future editions.

The Albert Einstein Archives, The Jewish National & University Library, The Hebrew University of Jerusalem, Israel from the essay *Wie ich die Welt sele* published in the English translation *Living Philosophies* 1930.

The Bertrand Russell research Centre for quotation by Bertrand Russell.

The Bhaktivedanta Book Trust from *The Bhagavad-Gita As It Is* by Prabhupada.

The Biblical quotations contained herein are used by permission from:
  The Revised Standard Version Bible, copyright © 1973, by the Division of Christian Education of the National council of the churches of Christ in the USA.
  The Revised English Bible © Oxford University Press and Cambridge University Press 1989.
  The New English Bible © Oxford University Press and Cambridge University Press 1961,1970.

Clear Point Press from *Taking The Bodhisattva Vow* by Bokar Rinpoche translated by Christine Buchet 1997.

Darton Longman and Todd Ltd and Doubleday, a division of Random House Inc. from *The New Jerusalem Bible* 1985.

Hodder and Stoughton Publishers from *Fear no Evil- a personal struggle with cancer* by David Watson 1984.

James Clarke from *Vol. II of The New Testament Apocrypha* edited by Wilhelm Schneemelcher.

The New Scientist from an article by Mark Hadley and an article by Charles Bennett.

Orion Publishing Group Ltd. from *Mapping The Mind* by Rita Carter.

Penguin Pitman and The Penguin Group (UK) from *The Collapse of Chaos*. © Jack Cohen and Ian Stewart 1994.

The Ramakrishna Vedanta Centre from The *Gospel of Ramakrishna, The Works of Swami Vivekananda* and Swami Nikhilanand's Commentary on *The Upanishads* based on the eighth century writings of Sri Sankaracharya.

Santa Fe Institute, from *Complexity to Perplexity* by John Horgen 1995 and from *Antichaos and Adaption* by Stuart Kauffman.

Scientific American January 1998 issue, from *The Architecture of Life* by Donald Ingber.

The Sikh Missionary Society from *Sri Guru Granth Sahib* Page 1.

About the Author

The author is a Chartered Engineer who started his career in the Ministry of Aviation and became involved in the design and management of many successful commercial projects in the communication, aircraft and computer world. He has now retired after spending many years as a principal lecturer and as an international consultant.

He was mainly educated at Surrey University and the University of Wales where he obtained his Master's Degree in Systems Engineering and his Doctorate in the field of Electromagnetics.

He has an abiding interest in many aspects of science, engineering, mathematics and the ramifications of the 'god phenomenon' which are found within all societies. For the past ten years his main interest has been centred on the daily reading of world scriptures, which has led to fruitful discussions with people of different faiths and to an involvement in various religious practices.

Michael, who is married with two grown up children, has retired to live in the Brecon Beacons National Park, Wales.